HAMLYN ALL COLOUR
BARBECUES &
SUMMER FOOD

HAMLYN ALL COLOUR
BARBECUES &
SUMMER FOOD

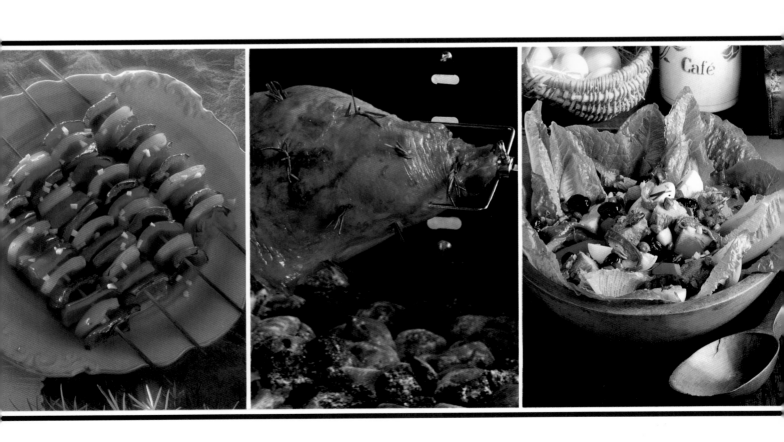

HAMLYN

Front cover shows, left to right:
Three pepper kebabs (recipe 137), Spit-roasted leg of lamb (recipe 69),
Salade Nicoise (recipe 161).

Back cover shows, clockwise from top left:
Barbecued marshmallows (recipe 213), Fruit punch (recipe 233), Bacon coils (recipe 1),
Red wine marinade (recipe 193), Italian fish bake (recipe 37).

First published in Great Britain 1994 by Hamlyn
an imprint of Reed Consumer Books Limited
Michelin House, 81 Fulham Road, London SW3 6RB
and Auckland, Melbourne, Singapore and Toronto.

Copyright © 1994 Reed International Books Limited

Line drawings by Lotta Heath
Photographs from Reed Consumer Books Picture Library

ISBN 0 600 58268 X

Recipes in this book were first published under other
Reed Consumer Books imprints.

A CIP catalogue record for this book is available from the British Library.

Produced by Mandarin Offset
Printed and bound in China

CONTENTS

USEFUL FACTS AND FIGURES

NOTES ON METRIFICATION

In this book quantities are given in metric and Imperial measures. Exact conversion from Imperial to metric measures does not usually give very convenient working quantities and so the metric measures have been rounded off into units of 25 grams. The table below shows the recommended equivalents.

Ounces	Approx g to nearest whole figure	Recommended conversion to nearest unit of 25	Ounces	Approx g to nearest whole figure	Recommended conversion to nearest unit of 25
1	28	25	9	255	250
2	57	50	10	283	275
3	85	75	11	312	300
4	113	100	12	340	350
5	142	150	13	368	375
6	170	175	14	396	400
7	198	200	15	425	425
8	227	225	16(1lb)	454	450

Note

When converting quantities over 16 oz first add the appropriate figures in the centre column, then adjust to the nearest unit of 25. As a general guide, 1kg (1000g) equals 2.2 lb or about 2 lb 3 oz. This method of conversion gives good results in nearly all cases, although in certain pastry and cake recipes a more accurate conversion is necessary to produce a balanced recipe.

Liquid measures

The millilitre has been used in this book and the following table gives a few examples.

Imperial	Approx ml to nearest whole figure	Recommended ml	Imperial	Approx ml to nearest whole figure	Recommended ml
1/4	142	150ml	1 pint	567	600 ml
1/2	238	300ml	1 1/2 pints	851	900 ml
3/4	425	450ml	1 1/4 pints	992	1000 ml (1 litre)

Spoon measures

All spoon measures given in this book are level unless otherwise stated.

Can sizes

At present, cans are marked with the exact (usually to the nearest whole number) metric equivalent of the Imperial weight of the contents, so we have followed this practice when giving can sizes.

Oven temperatures

The table below gives recommended equivalents.

	°C	°F	Gas Mark		°C	°F	Gas Mark
Very cool	110	225	1/4	Moderately hot	190	375	5
	120	250	1/2		200	400	6
Cool	140	275	1	Hot	220	425	7
	150	300	2		230	450	8
Moderate	160	325	3	Very Hot	240	475	9
	180	350	4				

NOTES FOR AMERICAN AND AUSTRALIAN USERS

In America the 8-fl oz measuring cup is used. In Australia metric measures are now used in conjunction with the standard 250-ml measuring cup. The Imperial pint, used in Britain and Australia, is 20 fl oz, while the American pint is 16 fl oz. It is important to remember that the Australian tablespoon differs from the British and American tablespoons; the table below gives a comparison. The British standard tablespoon, which has been used throughout this book, holds 17.7 ml, the American 14.2 ml, and the Australian 20 ml. A teaspoon holds approximately 5 ml in all three countries.

British	American	Australian
1 teaspoon	1 teaspoon	1 teaspoon
1 tablespoon	1 tablespoon	1 tablespoon
2 tablespoons	3 tablespoons	2 tablespoons
3 1/2 tablespoons	4 tablespoons	3 tablespoons
4 tablespoons	5 tablespoons	3 1/2 tablespoons

AN IMPERIAL/AMERICAN GUIDE TO SOLID AND LIQUID MEASURES

Imperial	American	Imperial	American
Solid measures		**Liquid measures**	
1 lb butter or margarine	2 cups	1/4 pint liquid	2/3 cup liquid
		1/2 pint	1 1/4 cups
1lb flour	4 cups	1/4 pint	2 cups
1 lb granulated or caster sugar	2 cups	1 pint	2 1/2 cups
		1 1/2 pints	3 3/4 cups
1 lb icing sugar	3 cups	2 pints	5 cups
8 oz rice	1 cup		(2 1/2 pints)

NOTE: WHEN MAKING ANY OF THE RECIPES IN THIS BOOK, ONLY FOLLOW ONE SET OF MEASURES AS THEY ARE NOT INTERCHANGEABLE.

INTRODUCTION

HAMLYN ALL COLOUR BARBECUES AND SUMMER FOOD is a compilation of 240 recipes, plus many ideas for varying the recipes, which allows you to enjoy outdoor cooking and outdoor eating to the full.

The book has recipes for food which may be cooked on all kinds of barbecue, from the simple to the elaborate. There are also many recipes for transportable food: food prepared and even cooked at home and then packed for taking on a picnic, or for cramming into a haversack.

There are recipes for all kinds of fish, meat and poultry, often marinated in delicious combinations of oils and flavourings. There is also a good selection of recipes for salads and vegetables, either hot or cold, for sauces, dips and marinades and for desserts and biscuits (for easy packing in the picnic hamper). The book ends with a small selection of recipes for thirst-quenching drinks.

All the features which have helped make the Hamlyn All Colour Cookbooks such good sellers are included in this new title in the series. Each recipe is photographed in colour, so that you can see at a glance how the dish will look when prepared and how it will fit into any menu you are planning. Preparation and cooking times for each recipe help make meal-planning easy and there is a calorie count, too. The Cook's Tip accompanying each recipe may suggest variations on the original recipe, describe unusual ingredients, or give hints on successful cooking, especially on a barbecue.

Whether you are buying a portable barbecue or building a permanent one, it is important to ensure that its cooking area will be big enough to cope with your family's needs. A grill area about 45 cm/18 inches across is big enough to cook food for eight people.

Special barbecue chips or briquettes are the best fuel for the barbecue. Remember that they need time to reach a good cooking heat before you put food on the grill. Adjust the cooking heat by raising or lowering the grill rack, and slow down the speed at which food is cooking by moving it to the side of the barbecue.

Among essential barbecue equipment are long-handled cooking implements, including tongs, fork, spoon and fish slice and a long-handled brush for basting food. A hinged wire grill is useful for foods, like fish, which break up easily and a flat baking sheet has various uses, including warming bread rolls. Have handy an oven glove and a sprinkler bottle for dowsing flames from dripping fat.

Successful picnics are very much a matter of advance planning, with a check list of essential items a must. As well as the usual freezer bag or insulated box to carry food safely and without damage, vacuum flasks for hot and cold drinks and soups, cutlery, plates and cups or glasses, the picnic bag should also contain empty plastic bags (for rubbish), insect repellant and a first aid kit, wet wipes or tissues and even a torch, if you think you may be packing up after sundown.

You will not need to pack HAMLYN ALL COLOUR BARBECUES AND SUMMER FOOD: it has been carefully planned to let you do as much advance preparation and cooking as possible. With it to hand, preparing summer food will be easy and relaxed.

STARTERS & SNACKS

Get summer meals off to a good start with the recipes here. There are delicious soups and elegant pâtés to start a dinner party or luncheon, fillings for picnic sandwiches, tarts and quiches for easy packing in a cool box or picnic hamper, and all sorts of delicious things to nibble on, from Bacon coils to barbecued spare ribs.

1   BACON COILS

Preparation time:	YOU WILL NEED:
25 minutes	750 g/ ½ lb streaky bacon,
	rinded
Cooking time:	350 g/12 oz sausagemeat
20 minutes	2 tablespoons finely chopped fresh
	parsley
Makes 24-26 coils	2 tablespoons finely chopped fresh
	chives
Calories:	2 anchovy fillets, pounded to a
128 - 118 per	paste
portion	freshly ground black pepper
	2 tablespoons wholegrain mustard

Lay the bacon slices out on a flat work surface and stretch each one slightly with the back of a large knife.

Put the sausagemeat in a large bowl, add the parsley, chives and anchovy paste and mix together thoroughly.

Sprinkle the bacon generously with pepper, then spread each slice with about 1/4 teaspoon of the mustard. Spread about 1 tablespoon of the sausagemeat mixture over each slice of bacon, then roll the slices up tightly and put on bamboo skewers, making sure the end of the bacon coil is held securely by the skewer.

Cook on the greased grill of a preheated barbecue for 20 minutes, turning the skewers every 5 minutes.

2   ICED SORREL SOUP

Preparation time:	YOU WILL NEED:
20 minutes, plus	6 tablespoons olive oil
cooling and	1 large onion, finely chopped
overnight chilling	1 kg/2 lb sorrel leaves, washed
	and trimmed of stalks, roughly
	chopped
Cooking time:	1 tablespoon grated orange rind
35 minutes	1 tablespoon lemon juice
	1.5 litres/2½ pints chicken stock
Serves 6	300 ml/½ pint double cream
	pinch of ground fenugreek
Calories:	salt and pepper
349 per portion	freshly grated nutmeg

Heat the oil in a large saucepan, add the onion and cook gently for 10 minutes. Add the sorrel leaves and cook for 3-4 minutes until they are a dark green colour, then add the orange rind, lemon juice and chicken stock. Bring to just below boiling point, then lower the heat and simmer gently for 15 minutes. Blend the soup in a liquidizer or food processor until smooth. Return to the rinsed pan and stir in the cream. Add the fenugreek, salt and black pepper and bring to the boil. Let it bubble for 4-5 minutes then remove from the heat and leave to cool.

When cool, transfer the soup to a bowl and chill overnight. Taste and adjust the seasoning. To take the soup to a picnic, pour it into a vacuum flask and transport in a cold box. Just before serving sprinkle generously with freshly grated nutmeg.

■ COOK'S TIP

The coils can be prepared up to 24 hours in advance, kept chilled and covered. Bring to room temperature before cooking. They may also be frozen up to 6 *weeks. Defrost in a cool place for 24 hours.*

■ COOK'S TIP

It is rare to see sorrel in the shops (except in France) so for this recipe you will have to grow your own. You will need 2-3 flourishing plants for the quantities above.

3   CREAM OF MUSHROOM SOUP

Preparation time:
15 minutes

Cooking time:
30 minutes

Serves 4

Calories:
498 per portion

YOU WILL NEED:
15 g/½ oz margarine or butter
1 small onion, finely chopped
225 g/8 oz mushrooms, finely
   chopped
1½ tablespoons plain flour
900 ml/1½ pints chicken stock
salt and pepper
pinch of grated nutmeg
1 bay leaf
150 ml/¼ pint single cream
1 tablespoon chopped fresh
   parsley, to garnish

Melt the margarine in a large saucepan. Add the onion and mushrooms, cover and cook gently for 5 minutes until soft. Stir in the flour and cook for a further 2 minutes, stirring constantly.

Gradually add the chicken stock and bring to the boil. Season to taste, add the nutmeg and bay leaf, lower the heat, half cover and simmer gently for about 20 minutes.

Remove from the heat, discard the bay leaf; stir in the cream. Garnish with parsley. Transport hot in a vacuum flask.

4   FENNEL SOUP

Preparation time:
15 minutes, plus
cooling and chilling
if serving the soup
cold

Cooking time:
45 minutes

Serves 6-8

Calories:
231 - 173 per portion

YOU WILL NEED:
2 large bulbs fennel, feathery
   leaves trimmed and
   reserved
5 tablespoons olive oil
2 litres/3½ pints chicken stock
150 ml/¼ pint double cream
1 teaspoon anisette or Pernod
salt and pepper
pinch of cayenne pepper

Wash the fennel and discard any damaged outer layers, then chop finely. Heat the oil in a large saucepan, add the fennel and cook very gently for 10 minutes, then pour in the chicken stock and bring to the boil. Lower the heat again, and simmer gently for 25 minutes until the fennel is softened.

Strain the soup through a large sieve into a jug. Add about two-thirds of the cooked fennel to the liquid and blend in a liquidizer until smooth.

Return the liquid to the pan and add the reserved fennel pieces. Stir in the double cream, anisette or Pernod and bring to just below boiling point, stirring once or twice.

Season with salt and a generous sprinkling of freshly ground black pepper. If serving immediately, pour into a warmed soup tureen. To serve the soup cold, cool and chill for about 1 hour. Garnish with the reserved fennel leaves, sprinkle with cayenne pepper and serve.

◾ COOK'S TIP

Serve this soup with crusty wholemeal bread. You could also serve this soup chilled with a garnish of chives instead of parsley.

◾ COOK'S TIP

Homemade chicken stock has a more subtle flavour than stock made with cubes, but the latter can be substituted if necessary.

5 PATE-STUFFED HAM WITH TOMATO AND BASIL

Preparation time:
25 minutes

Serves 6

Calories:
255 per portion

YOU WILL NEED:
225 g/8 oz pâté de foie gras
6 thin slices of smoked ham
2 beefsteak tomatoes, finely sliced
3 tablespoons shredded fresh basil
    leaves
6 tablespoons olive oil
1½ tablespoons tarragon vinegar
¼ teaspoon Dijon mustard
pinch of brown sugar
salt and pepper

If using canned pâté, turn it into a bowl and mash lightly, then divide into 6 portions and shape each into a long thin roll.

Put a portion of the pâté at one end of each slice of ham and roll up. Set aside.

Spread the tomato slices over 6 individual serving plates and sprinkle with the basil.

Mix together the olive oil, vinegar, mustard and brown sugar and whisk until thickened. Pour a little of the dressing over each plate, then place a ham 'roll' in the centre of the plate. Sprinkle a little salt over the tomatoes, then season with freshly ground black pepper and serve.

6 CHILLED TOMATO AND ORANGE SOUP

Preparation time:
15 minutes

Cooking time:
1 hour 10 minutes

Serves 4-6

Calories:
183 - 122 per portion

YOU WILL NEED:
25 g/1 oz margarine or butter
100 g/4 oz red lentils
1 carrot, chopped
1 large onion, chopped
thinly pared rind and juice of 1
    orange
750 g/1½ lb tomatoes, skinned
    and chopped
1 bay leaf
900 ml/1½ pints chicken stock
salt and pepper
1 tablespoon snipped chives, to
    garnish

Melt the margarine in a large saucepan. Add the lentils, carrot and onion and fry over a gentle heat for about 5 minutes until softened, stirring occasionally.

Add the orange rind to the pan with the tomatoes and bay leaf. Pour in the stock, season to taste, then bring to the boil. Cover and simmer for 1 hour, or until all the ingredients are soft.

Discard the bay leaf, then purée the soup in a liquidizer or press through a sieve. Stir in the orange juice and adjust the seasoning to taste.

Chill the soup for at least 2 hours. Stir in a little extra cold chicken stock if it is too thick, adjust the seasoning to taste and garnish with chives. Transport in a vacuum flask.

■ COOK'S TIP

As an alternative to the expensive pâté de fois gras use the more economical Chicken liver, port and pistachio terrine (recipe 10), making it without the nuts.

■ COOK'S TIP

Serve the soup with french bread. If you have no lentils, use a diced potato instead when preparing the soup.

7 CREAMY AVOCADO PATE

Preparation time:
10 minutes

Serves 4

Calories:
326 per portion

YOU WILL NEED:
2 avocados, halved and stoned
4 hard-boiled eggs, finely chopped
2 tablespoons cider or red wine
vinegar
1 garlic clove, finely chopped
2 teaspoons finely chopped fresh
lemon balm
salt and pepper
8 lettuce leaves,
4 parsley sprigs, to garnish

Carefully scoop out the avocado flesh, leaving the skins intact and put the flesh in a mixing bowl. Reserve the skins. Mash the avocado flesh with the eggs, vinegar, garlic, lemon balm, salt and pepper to a smooth paste. Spoon the mixture back into the avocado skins.

Arrange the lettuce leaves on four individual serving plates. Top each with an avocado half. Garnish each portion with a sprig of parsley. Serve at once.

8 TUNA PATE

Preparation time:
10 minutes

Serves 8

Calories:
159 per portion

YOU WILL NEED:
100 g/4 oz butter, melted
2 garlic cloves, crushed
2 x 200 g/7 oz cans tuna fish,
drained
2 tablespoons olive oil
1 tablespoon lemon juice
salt and pepper
chopped parsley, to garnish

Mix together the butter and garlic. Roughly flake the tuna fish and place half in a blender goblet with half the melted butter mixture and 1 tablespoon of the olive oil. Blend until smooth. Remove and blend the remaining fish with the remaining butter mixture and olive oil. Mix all the blended fish together and stir in the lemon juice and salt and pepper to taste. Spoon into a serving dish and garnish with chopped parsley. Cover with foil or cling film and chill.

▦ COOK'S TIP

Lemon balm (often simply called balm) is a herb with a lemony scent. Available fresh or dried, it is used in salads (fruit and vegetable), soups, sauces and drinks.

▦ COOK'S TIP

If this pâté is to be taken on a picnic, spoon it straight into a lidded plastic storage box before chilling it. It will then be very easy to pack and transport.

9 TARAMASALATA

Preparation time:
20 minutes

Serves 6

Calories:
167 per portion

YOU WILL NEED:
1 slice of white bread, crusts removed
4 tablespoons olive oil
1-2 garlic cloves
225 g/8 oz smoked cod's roe
1 small potato, cooked and peeled
lemon juice
2-3 fresh parsley sprigs
2 tablespoons cold water
salt and pepper
FOR THE GARNISH
lemon wedges
black olives

Soak the bread in cold water. Squeeze dry. Pour the oil into a blender goblet and add the garlic, cod's roe, potato, lemon juice to taste, bread and parsley. Blend until smooth. (A better consistency is obtained if the ingredients are added a little at a time.) Thin with a little of the cold water if the mixture seems too stiff to blend. Add salt and pepper to taste, then stir in the remaining water to give a soft, creamy consistency.

Pour into a bowl or rigid plastic box and smooth the top. Cover with foil or cling film and chill. Serve garnished with lemon wedges and black olives.

10 CHICKEN LIVER, PORT AND PISTACHIO TERRINE

Preparation time:
15 minutes, plus chilling overnight

Cooking time:
5 minutes

Serves 6-8

Calories:
185 - 139 per portion

YOU WILL NEED:
120 g/4½ oz butter
350 g/12 oz chicken livers, all yellowish bits removed
1 teaspoon juniper berries, crushed
1 mace blade, crumbled
¼ teaspoon ground allspice
1 garlic clove, crushed
4 tablespoons port
salt and pepper
50 g/2 oz shelled pistachio nuts, halved
120 ml/4 fl oz clarified butter (see Cook's Tip)

Melt 50 g/2 oz of the butter in a frying-pan. When beginning to bubble add the chicken livers. Cook them, stirring, for 4-5 minutes until they are firm but still pink inside. Remove the livers from the pan. Add the juniper berries, mace, allspice, garlic and port to the pan. Allow to bubble for 1 minute then pour over the chicken livers, scraping up any sediment from the bottom of the pan with a spatula.

Blend the chicken livers to a purée. Season well. Add the rest of the butter and beat well together, then put half the mixture into a serving bowl. Reserve about 15 of the pistachio nuts, then scatter the rest over the chicken liver pâté. Cover with the remaining pâté, then push the reserved nuts into the top of the pâté at an angle, leaving just the tips exposed.

■ COOK'S TIP

Taramasalata is a Greek speciality; for an authentic touch, serve it with a Greek style bread, such as pitta bread.

■ COOK'S TIP

To make about 100 g/4 oz clarified butter, melt 175 g/6 oz unsalted butter in a pan until dissolved and just beginning to bubble. Remove from the heat and *strain into a bowl. The white sediment is strained off to leave a clear yellow liquid which can be kept, chilled, up to 1 week and used as required.*

11 WHOLEMEAL SCOTCH EGGS

Preparation time:
20 minutes

Cooking time:
10 minutes

Serves 4

Calories:
375 per portion

YOU WILL NEED:
5 eggs
25 g/1 oz plain flour
salt and pepper
225 g/8 oz pork sausagemeat
50 g/2 oz wholemeal
breadcrumbs, toasted, for coating
vegetable oil, for deep frying

Hard-boil 4 of the eggs. Drain, plunge into cold water and leave to cool, then shell. Season the flour with salt and pepper and use to coat the hard-boiled eggs.

Divide the sausagemeat into 4 equal portions and on a floured board or work surface roll each piece into a circle large enough to cover an egg completely.

Place 1 egg in the centre of each sausagemeat circle and carefully mould the sausagemeat round the egg. Pinch the edges firmly together, to seal.

Beat the remaining egg and use to coat the Scotch eggs, then roll in the breadcrumbs, until thoroughly coated.

Heat the oil in a deep fat fryer to 170 C/340 F or until a stale bread cube browns in 60 seconds, and deep fry the Scotch eggs for about 8 minutes until crisp and lightly browned. Drain on absorbent kitchen paper and leave to cool. Transport wrapped individually in foil or cling film, in a rigid container.

12 WELSH PICNIC FLANS

Preparation time:
25 minutes

Cooking time:
about 20 minutes

Oven temperature:
180 C/350 F/gas 4

Serves 10-12

Calories:
361 - 301 per portion

YOU WILL NEED:
450 g/1 lb shortcrust pastry
50 g/2 oz butter
5 large leeks, sliced
1 teaspoon dried oregano
5 eggs
300 ml/½ pint single cream
salt and pepper
1 tablespoon chopped fresh parsley

Roll out the pastry dough and use to line six 11.5 cm/4½ inch diameter flan rings and one 20 cm/8 inch diameter flan ring. Bake blind for 20 minutes (see Cook's Tip) and allow to cool. Melt the butter in a frying pan. Add the leeks and fry gently until transparent. Remove from the heat and allow to cool. Sprinkle over the oregano and divide between the pastry shells.

Beat together the eggs, cream and salt and pepper to taste and pour over the leeks. Sprinkle with the chopped parsley. Bake in a preheated moderate oven for 20 minutes. Allow to cool, then cover individual flans with cling film and place in rigid containers for easy carrying.

■ COOK'S TIP

Add ½ teaspoon dried sage to the sausagemeat for a deliciously herby Scotch egg.

■ COOK'S TIP

To bake the flan cases blind, place a piece of greaseproof paper on the pastry and fill with baking beans (or rice, which may be kept and used again for *the purpose). Bake in a moderately hot oven (200 C/400 F/gas 6).*

13 CURRIED CHICKEN TARTLETS

Preparation time:
20 minutes

Cooking time:
15 minutes

Oven temperature:
200 C/400 F/gas 6

Serves 4

Calories:
677 per portion

YOU WILL NEED:
175 g/6 oz shortcrust pastry
2 teaspoons curry powder
2 tablespoons lemon juice
100 g/4 oz walnuts, roughly
    chopped
350 g/12 oz cooked chicken meat,
    cut into thin strips
120 ml/4-5 fl oz mayonnaise
salt and pepper
chopped fresh parsley

Divide the pastry dough into four. Roll out each piece and use to line four 11.5 cm/4½ inch diameter tartlet cases. Bake blind for 15 minutes (see recipe 12) and allow to cool.

Stir the curry powder, lemon juice, walnuts and chicken into the mayonnaise and season to taste with salt and pepper. Spoon into the tartlet cases and sprinkle with chopped parsley. Cover with cling film and store in the refrigerator until the last moment. Place in a rigid plastic container for easy carrying.

14 CUMBERLAND PIE

Preparation time:
20 minutes

Cooking time:
25-35 minutes

Oven temperature:
220 C/425 F/gas 7,
then
160 C/325 F/gas 3

Serves 4

Calories:
634 per portion

YOU WILL NEED:
1 x 212 g/7½ oz packet frozen
    puff pastry, thawed
500 g/1 lb pork sausagemeat
2 bacon rashers, rinds removed,
    diced
large pinch of died sage or thyme
salt and pepper
4 eggs
1 tablespoon chopped fresh parsley

Roll out two-thirds of the pastry and use to line a 20 cm/8 inch diameter flan ring. Do not trim away the surplus dough.

Cook the sausagemeat and bacon to remove excess fat. Drain and allow to cool, then place in the pastry case. Sprinkle with the sage or thyme, salt and pepper. Make four indentations in the meat and break an egg into each one. Sprinkle over the parsley. Roll out the remaining dough and dampen the edges. Use to cover the pie. Press down the edges and trim away the excess dough. Glaze with the egg white remaining in the shells.

Bake in a preheated hot oven for 15 minutes, then reduce the heat to moderate and bake for a further 10-15 minutes. Allow to cool, then wrap in foil or carry in a rigid plastic box.

■ COOK'S TIP

To make your own rich shortcrust pastry, sift together 175 g/6 oz plain flour and a pinch of salt. Rub in 100 g/4 oz hard margarine or butter until the mixture resembles fine breadcrumbs. Bind together with 1 egg yolk and 1 tablespoon cold water. Chill 20 minutes before rolling out.

■ COOK'S TIP

Slip a bottle of tomato ketchup into the picnic basket to make an excellent accompaniment for this easily transported pie.

15 SAUSAGE AND APPLE TURNOVERS

Preparation time:
30 minutes

Cooking time:
30-40 minutes

Oven temperature:
200 C/400 F/gas 6

Serves 8

Calories:
625 per portion

YOU WILL NEED:
2 x 375 g/13 oz packets frozen
    puff pastry, thawed
225 g/8 oz canned unsweetened
    apple purée
450 g/1 lb sausagemeat
100 g/4 oz Cheddar cheese, grated
1 teaspoon Worcestershire sauce
1 egg, beaten
salt and pepper
milk, for brushing
1 egg yolk, beaten, to glaze

Roll out the pastry into 2 oblongs about 40 x 20 cm/16 x 8 inches. Cut each oblong in half to make 2 squares then cut each square into 4 triangles (16 triangles in all). Dampen a baking sheet and lay 8 triangles on it. Spread a little apple purée on each triangle, leaving a 1 cm/½ inch border all round.

Mix the sausagemeat with the cheese, Worcestershire sauce, egg, salt and pepper. Divide the mixture into 8 portions, roll into balls then flatten into rough triangle shapes. Place on top of the apple purée. Brush the edges of all the triangles with a little milk, then place another triangle on top, pressing the edges with the fingertips to seal well. Make a slit in the top of each turnover, then brush the tops with the beaten egg yolk.

Bake for 30-40 minutes until the tops are golden.

■ COOK'S TIP

To give the turnovers a more sophisticated flavour, add a sautéed onion, a few crushed juniper berries and a drop or two of Tabasco sauce to the sausagemeat.

16 CURRIED PRAWN TARTLETS

Preparation time:
25 minutes, plus
chilling

Cooking time:
25-30 minutes

Oven temperature:
190 C/375 F/gas 5

Makes 10

Calories:
178 per portion

YOU WILL NEED:
175 g/6 oz plain flour
pinch of salt
40 g/1½ oz lard
40 g/1½ oz block margarine, diced
2-3 tablespoons cold water
FOR THE FILLING
25 g/1 oz margarine or butter
25 g/1 oz plain flour
1 teaspoon curry paste
300 ml/½ pint milk
few drops anchovy essence
225 g/8 oz peeled prawns
salt and pepper

Sift the flour with the salt, add the fats and rub in. Using a round-bladed knife, mix in enough cold water to bind, then knead lightly, wrap in cling film and chill.

Melt the margarine in a saucepan, then stir in the flour and curry paste over a low heat. Cook, stirring, for 2-3 minutes, then remove from the heat and gradually stir in the milk. Return the saucepan to the heat and bring gently to simmering point, stirring. Simmer 4-5 minutes, then stir in the anchovy essence. Pour the sauce into a bowl, cover and leave to cool.

Roll out the pastry and cut into 10 rounds, using a 7.5 cm/3 inch fluted pastry cutter. Press the rounds into tartlet tins, prick the bases and bake for 15-20 minutes until crisp and golden. Transfer the tartlet cases to a wire rack to cool.

When the curry sauce is cold, stir in the prawns, with salt and pepper. Fill the cold pastry cases with the mixture.

■ COOK'S TIP

Add 75 g/3 oz grated Gruyère cheese to the sauce after stirring in the milk. The completed tartlets could be garnished with prawns (reserve a few from the filling), parsley sprigs and a shake of paprika, if liked.

17 CHEESE AND ONION TARTS

Preparation time: 20 minutes	YOU WILL NEED: 100 g/4 oz plain flour *pinch of salt*
Cooking time: 35-40 minutes	*25 g/1 oz block margarine or butter, diced* *25 g/1 oz lard, diced* *1-2 tablespoons water*
Oven temperature: 190 C/375 F/gas 5	*FOR THE FILLING* *15 g/½ oz margarine or butter*
Serves 4	*1 onion, chopped* *1 dessert apple, peeled, cored and grated* *50 g/2 oz mature Cheddar cheese, grated*
Calories: 354 per portion	*1 egg* *about 100 ml/3½ fl oz milk* *salt and pepper*

Make the pastry as for Curried prawn tartlets (recipe 16).

Divide the dough into 4 equal portions. Roll each portion out and use to line four 10 cm/4 inch tart tins.

To make the filling, melt the margarine in a small frying pan, add the onion and fry gently for 5 minutes until soft and lightly coloured. Divide the onion equally among the pastry cases and cover with the apple and cheese.

Beat the egg in a measuring jug and make up to 150 ml/¼ pint with milk. Season and pour into the pastry cases.

Bake the tarts in a preheated oven for 30-35 minutes or until the filling is set and golden. Remove from the oven and leave to cool for a few minutes in the tins, then transfer to a wire rack to cool completely.

■ COOK'S TIP

For an increased savoury flavour, use 2 slices cooked ham, chopped, instead of the apple in the filling.

18 CHICKEN PASTIES

Preparation time: 15 minutes, plus chilling	YOU WILL NEED: *225 g/8 oz self-raising flour* *1 teaspoon salt* *50 g/2 oz lard, diced*
Cooking time: 35-40 minutes	*50 g/2 oz block margarine, diced* *3-4 tablespoons water* *beaten egg, to glaze*
Oven temperature: 200 C/400 F/gas 6	*FOR THE FILLING* *1 x 198 g/7 oz can asparagus tips, drained and chopped, liquid reserved*
Serves 4	*milk*
Calories: 583 per portion	*15 g/½ margarine or butter* *1 tablespoon plain flour* *225 g/8 oz boneless cooked chicken, skinned and chopped* *salt and pepper*

Make the pastry dough as for Curried prawn tartlets (recipe 16). Wrap in cling film and chill.

Make the asparagus liquid up to 150 ml/¼ pint with milk.

Melt the margarine in a pan, stir in the flour and cook over low heat for 1 minute. Gradually stir in the liquid mixture and bring to the boil, stirring, until thickened. Take off the heat and add the chicken, asparagus and salt and pepper.

Roll out the dough and cut four 18 cm/7 inch rounds, using a plate as guide. Spoon a portion of filling on to each round, dampen the edges, form into a semi-circle and seal and flute the edges firmly. Brush the pasties with egg and bake for about 30 minutes until golden brown.

■ COOK'S TIP

Since these pasties are quite crisp, protect them for transporting to a picnic by wrapping them in double-thickness foil.

19 SPINACH QUICHE

Preparation time:
15 minutes, plus
chilling

Cooking time:
40-45 minutes

Oven temperature:
190 C/375 F/gas 5

Serves 4

Calories:
538 per portion

YOU WILL NEED:
150 g/6 oz plain wholemeal flour
pinch of salt
75 g/3 oz block margarine or
    butter, diced
2-3 tablespoons water
25 g/1 oz Parmesan cheese, grated
FOR THE FILLING
450 g/1 lb spinach
50 g/2 oz Cheddar cheese, grated
142 ml/5 fl oz carton single cream
2 eggs
½ teaspoon grated nutmeg
salt and pepper

To make the pastry, sift the flour with the salt into a mixing bowl and tip in the bran from the sieve. Add the margarine and rub in. Using a round-bladed knife, mix in enough water to make a firm dough. Turn the dough on to a floured board and knead lightly. Roll out and use to line a 20 cm/8 inch flan tin. Chill in the refrigerator while preparing the filling.

Wash the spinach, discarding the stalks and any tough leaves. Place in a saucepan, cover and simmer over moderate heat, with no added water, for about 5 minutes or until tender. Drain and chop finely. Place in a bowl and add the remaining filling ingredients. Beat well until thoroughly blended and pour into the chilled flan case.

Sprinkle the Parmesan cheese over the top and bake the quiche for 35 minutes or until firm and golden. Remove from the oven and leave until cold

20 HAM AND TOMATO FILLING

Preparation time:
10 minutes

Serves 2

Calories:
460 per portion

YOU WILL NEED:
2 slices cooked ham, finely chopped
2 tomatoes, skinned and finely
    chopped
100 g/4 oz butter, softened
salt and pepper

Mix together the ham, tomato and butter and season to taste with salt and pepper.

This amount will fill 2 rounds of sandwiches (i.e. 4 sandwiches) or 4 bread rolls.

■ COOK'S TIP

For a variation on this recipe, sprinkle the pastry base with 4 rashers streaky bacon, lightly fried and chopped, before adding the spinach filling.

■ COOK'S TIP

Since this is quite a wet filling, which could make sandwiches soggy, it would be a good idea to transport it to a picnic in a plastic box, filling the sandwich *bread or rolls when they are wanted.*

21 COTTAGE CHEESE AND CHIVE FILLING

Preparation time:
5 minutes

Serves 2

Calories:
266 per portion

YOU WILL NEED:
50 g/2 oz butter, softened
100 g/4 oz cottage cheese
1 teaspoon chopped fresh chives

Cream the butter, cottage cheese and chives thoroughly together and chill before using.

This amount will fill 2 rounds of sandwiches (i.e. 4 sandwiches) or 4 bread rolls.

22 TUNA AND TOMATO FILLING

Preparation time:
5 minutes

Serves 8

Calories:
82 per portion

YOU WILL NEED:
7 oz can tuna fish, drained and
flaked
2 teaspoons vinegar
2 tablespoons tomato ketchup
2 tomatoes, skinned and finely
chopped
salt and pepper
50 g/2 oz butter, softened

Mix together the tuna fish, vinegar, tomato ketchup and tomatoes. Add salt and pepper to taste, then combine with the butter.

This quantity will fill 3 rounds of sandwiches (i.e. 6 sandwiches) or 6 rolls.

■ COOK'S TIP

If liked, treat this filling like a savoury butter, spreading it on the bread and adding extra ingredients, such as chopped celery or carrot, nuts or chopped ham.

■ COOK'S TIP

Use either tuna in brine or in olive oil for this recipe. Tuna in brine has fewer calories, but the olive oil flavour blends well with the tomatoes.

23 MOZZARELLA AND SALAMI-STUFFED BREAD

Preparation time:
5 minutes

Cooking time:
20 minutes

Serves 4-8

Calories:
396 - 198 per portion

YOU WILL NEED:
1 large French bread stick
100 g/4 oz mozzarella cheese
stoned black olives
50 g/2 oz sliced salami

Using a sharp knife, cut the bread into thick slices without cutting right through the bread. Cut the mozzarella and olives into thin slices. Insert a slice each of mozzarella and salami and an olive between each bread slice.

Wrap the loaf in a large sheet of buttered foil and seal tightly. Place over hot coals and heat for 10 minutes on each side. Unwrap and cut between the slices before serving.

24 CUCUMBER AND CELERY FILLING

Preparation time:
5 minutes

Serves 3

Calories:
286 per portion

YOU WILL NEED:
100g/4 oz butter, softened
1 x 5 cm/2 inch piece cucumber,
  peeled and very finely chopped
1 large celery stalk, very finely
  chopped
salt and pepper

Beat together the butter, cucumber and celery. Add salt and pepper to taste and mix well.

This amount will fill 6 sandwiches (i.e. 3 rounds) or 6 rolls.

■ COOK'S TIP

Almost like a pizza, this is irresistible and makes a good starter to nibble while the main course is cooking on the barbecue.

■ COOK'S TIP

This filling has a deliciously cool, delicate flavour; to give it an extra tang, add chopped fresh mint or chives to taste.

25 HOT DOGS

Preparation time:
5 minutes

Cooking time:
5-8 minutes

Serves 4

Calories:
485 per portion

YOU WILL NEED:
4 large frankfurter sausages
4 long bread rolls or pieces of
    French bread
4 tablespoons tomato ketchup
    (optional)

Lightly prick the frankfurters. Place directly on the grill and cook, over medium coals, for 5-8 minutes, turning frequently.

Place the bread rolls on a board and cut carefully without going right through the bread, leaving it 'hinged' at the back.

Using tongs or a fork, place a frankfurter in each roll. Spoon over a little of the tomato ketchup, if liked. Serve in soft paper napkins while still warm.

26 LAYERED SANDWICH LOAF

Preparation time:
15 minutes

Cooking time:
about 5 minutes

Serves 4-6

Calories:
751 - 501 per portion

YOU WILL NEED:
1 x 18 cm/7 inch round granary or
    wholemeal loaf
butter, softened for spreading
FOR THE EGG FILLING
3 eggs, beaten
1 tablespoon milk
15 g/½ oz butter
salt and pepper
3 spring onions, finely chopped
FOR THE CHICKEN FILLING
175 g/6 oz cooked chicken, minced
1 celery stalk, thinly sliced
2-3 tablespoons thick mayonnaise
1 teaspoon curry paste
FOR THE CHEESE FILLING
175 g/6 oz Cheddar cheese, grated
2 tomatoes, skinned and chopped

First make the fillings. Cook the eggs, milk, butter and salt and pepper over gentle heat, stirring, until scrambled but still creamy. Take off the heat, add the spring onions and let cool.

Put the chicken and celery in a bowl and stir in mayonnaise to give a spreading consistency. Add curry paste to taste.

Mix the cheese with the tomato.

Cut the loaf horizontally into 4 layers. Butter each cut surface. Spread a layer with each filling and reassemble the loaf. Wrap in foil until required. To serve, unwrap and slice vertically.

■ COOK'S TIP

Other sauces to have on hand could include a mustard sauce or thick barbecue sauce such as recipe 198.

■ COOK'S TIP

Vary the filling layers. Try egg and ham mayonnaise, tuna and onion, minced pork with apple and salad cream, or garlic sausage with spring onion tops.

27 TUNA-STUFFED TOMATOES

Preparation time:
10 minutes

Serves 4

Calories:
69 per portion

YOU WILL NEED:
1 x 200 g/7 oz can tuna, drained
  and flaked
1 medium celery stalk, chopped
2 tablespoons finely chopped
  onion
2 tablespoons finely chopped
  green pepper
3 tablespoons French dressing
salt and pepper
4 large tomatoes
6 lettuce leaves
4 lemon slices, to garnish

Mix together the tuna, celery, onion, green pepper, dressing and salt and pepper to taste. Chill.

With stem end down, cut each tomato into six wedges, cutting down to, but not through, the base. Spread the wedges apart slightly and sprinkle lightly with salt. Place the lettuce leaves on a serving plate. Put the tomatoes on the lettuce. Spoon equal amounts of the tuna mixture into the centre of each tomato. Garnish with twists of lemon and serve.

COOK'S TIP

This makes a pretty and substantial first course; or serve it with a salad or wholemeal bread for a cool lunch-time snack.

28 SMOKED HADDOCK ROLLS

Preparation time:
30 minutes

Cooking time:
25 minutes

Serves 8

Calories:
620 per portion

YOU WILL NEED:
750 g/1½ lb smoked haddock
750 ml/1¼ pints milk
1 teaspoon paprika pepper
5 tablespoons mayonnaise
freshly ground black pepper
1 tablespoon lemon juice
16 tablespoons olive oil
8 soft rolls, halved
4 ripe but firm avocados
salt
4 teaspoons tarragon vinegar
4 tablespoons finely chopped fresh
  parsley
32 slices of lemon

Rinse the haddock, put it in a pan and cover with the milk. Bring to the boil and simmer for 25 minutes. Take the fish out of the pan, then skin and flake it, removing as many bones as possible. Strain the milk stock and reserve 6 tablespoons.

Mash the fish with the paprika, mayonnaise, black pepper, lemon juice and half the reserved stock. If the mixture seems a little thick, add some more of the stock. It should be creamy in consistency without being too thin.

Dribble a tablespoon of oil over the cut side of each roll. Halve, stone and peel the avocados, then slice them. Arrange a layer of slices on each roll half. Sprinkle with a small pinch of salt and dribble ¼ teaspoon vinegar over the avocado slices.

Spread the fish mixture over the avocados, making sure they are completely covered so they do not discolour. Sprinkle a little parsley on top, then cover with 2 slices of lemon.

COOK'S TIP

The rolls may be prepared up to 18 hours in advance and chilled, covered in clingfilm, until required. Bring to cool room temperature before eating.

29   SPARE RIBS WITH A BARBECUE SAUCE

Preparation time:	YOU WILL NEED:
10 minutes	12-16 pork spare ribs
	2 tablespoons clear honey
Cooking time:	3 tablespoons soy sauce
45 minutes	3 tablespoons tomato ketchup
	Tabasco sauce
Oven temperature:	1 small garlic clove, crushed
180 C/350 F/gas 4	dry mustard
	paprika
Serves 4	salt and pepper
	4 tablespoons orange juice
Calories:	4 tablespoons wine vinegar
383 per portion	

If not already done, separate the meat into individual ribs. Cook under a preheated moderate grill for 15 minutes or until brown, turning several times. Arrange in a single layer in a roasting tin.

For the barbecue sauce, mix together the honey, soy sauce, tomato ketchup, a few drops of Tabasco, the garlic and mustard, paprika, salt and pepper to taste. Stir in the orange juice and vinegar. Pour over the spare ribs.

Cook, uncovered, in a preheated moderate oven for 30 minutes. Serve piping hot in the sauce.

30   CHINESE BARBECUED SPARE RIBS

Preparation time:	YOU WILL NEED:
15 minutes, plus	1.5 kg/3 lb spare ribs, separated
marinating	between the bones
	salt and pepper
Cooking time:	FOR THE CHINESE MARINADE
45 minutes	4 tablespoons hoisin sauce
	2 tablespoons clear honey
Serves 4-6	4 tablespoons soy sauce
	4 teaspoons wine vinegar
Calories:	8 tablespoons chicken stock
595 - 397 per portion	¼ teaspoon Chinese five spice
	powder

First, make the marinade. Put all the ingredients in a bowl or jug and stir together briskly. Rub the spare ribs all over with a little salt, then sprinkle generously with freshly ground black pepper and place in a shallow dish.

Pour over the marinade, cover and leave in a cool place for 4 hours, turning the ribs half way through.

Drain the marinade into a jug and put the spare ribs into a hinged wire grill (this makes turning the ribs a much quicker operation) and cook on the greased grill of a preheated barbecue for 10 minutes, then turn and cook for a further 10 minutes.

Baste the top side of the ribs with the marinade, turn again and cook for 15 minutes, then baste and turn again, cooking for a final 10 minutes.

■ COOK'S TIP

This recipe assumes the barbecue grill is full! Because the ribs do not need marinating, they are quick to cook and serve.

■ COOK'S TIP

The ingredients for this marinade are sold by large supermarkets. The marinade will keep in a screw-topped jar in the refrigerator for one week.

31 BRUNCH SKEWERS

Preparation time:
15 minutes

Cooking time:
10 minutes

Serves 4

Calories:
328 per portion

YOU WILL NEED:
*175 g/6 oz streaky bacon rashers,
    rinded*
4 small tomatoes
16 cocktail sausages
*4 lambs' kidneys, skinned, halved
    and cored*
2 tablespoons vegetable oil
salt and pepper
watercress sprigs, to garnish

Lay the bacon rashers on a board and stretch them with the back of a knife. Cut in half crossways and roll up.

Slice the tomatoes in half; thread one half on to each skewer to begin.

Thread the bacon rolls and sausages alternately with the kidney halves on to 4 oiled kebab skewers. Finish each skewer with a tomato half.

Brush the skewered meats with oil, season to taste with salt and pepper, and cook on a hot barbecue for 10 minutes, turning once, or until well browned and cooked through. Garnish the skewers with sprigs of watercress.

32 BARBECUED SPARE RIBS

Preparation time:
10 minutes, plus
cooling

Cooking time:
25-30 minutes

Serves 4

Calories:
312 per portion

YOU WILL NEED:
1 kg/2 lb pork spare ribs
1 tablespoon red wine vinegar
salt
fresh parsley, to garnish
FOR THE SAUCE
2 tablespoons tomato ketchup
2 tablespoons clear honey
2 tablespoons soy sauce
2 tablespoons red wine vinegar
*½ teaspoon English mustard
    powder*
65 ml/2 ½ fl oz water
2 teaspoons Worcestershire sauce
½ teaspoon paprika
salt and pepper

Place the spare ribs and vinegar in a large saucepan of salted water. Bring to the boil, then simmer for 15 minutes.

Meanwhile, place all the sauce ingredients in a saucepan; stir well. Bring to the boil, then lower the heat and simmer for 5 minutes.

Strain the spare ribs, place in a large bowl and pour over the sauce. Leave until cool, turning frequently.

Remove the spare ribs, reserving the sauce. Cook the spare ribs on a hot barbecue, turning once, for 10-15 minutes, until crisp and brown.

Serve garnished with fresh parsley; reheat the sauce and hand round separately with the spare ribs.

■ COOK'S TIP

Serve these skewers with scrambled eggs as an accompanying dish for a hearty breakfast treat. They could also be served with warm wholemeal or *pumpernickel rolls and butter for a tempting supper dish.*

■ COOK'S TIP

Other pork cuts which barbecue deliciously with this sauce include whole fillets (tenderloin) and spare rib and loin chops.

33 ORIENTAL SPARE RIBS

Preparation time:	YOU WILL NEED:
10 minutes	*750 g/1½ lb pork spareribs*
	5-mm/½-in piece root ginger
Cooking time:	*2 tablespoons oil*
45-60 minutes	*2 garlic cloves, crushed*
	1 green pepper
Serves 4-6	*pinch of five-spice powder*
	1 tablespoon soy sauce
Calories:	*2 tablespoons dry sherry*
249 - 166 per portion	*2 tablespoons tomato purée*
	2 tablespoons vinegar
	2 tablespoons honey

Cut the pork into individual ribs. Cook in boiling water for 10 minutes, then drain well. Peel and grate the ginger; chop the pepper, discarding the core and seeds. Heat the oil in a frying pan and fry the garlic, ginger, pepper and five-spice powder together for 2-3 minutes. Add the remaining ingredients and stir well. Simmer for 5 minutes. Brush over the ribs and cook them over hot coals for 6-8 minutes on each side. Move the ribs to warm coals and continue grilling for a further 20-30 minutes, brushing frequently with the marinade. Serve with rice and spring onion tassels.

34 MINT, POPPY AND SESAME KEBABS

Preparation time:	YOU WILL NEED:
35 minutes	*350 g/12 oz lean lamb, minced*
	350 g/12 oz rump steak, minced
Cooking time:	*350 g/12 oz lean pork, minced*
10-12 minutes	*1 large onion, grated*
	salt and pepper
Serves 4-6	*3 garlic cloves, crushed*
	3 tablespoons Dijon mustard
Calories:	*1½ tablespoons coriander seeds,*
536 - 357 per portion	*crushed*
	9 tablespoons finely chopped fresh
	* mint*
	6 tablespoons poppy seeds
	9 tablespoons sesame seeds, toasted

Put each of the minced meats into a separate bowl and add some grated onion, salt and black pepper to each.

To the lamb add the garlic, to the beef add the mustard, and to the pork add the coriander seeds. Mix the meats and seasonings well, then divide each mixture into 8 balls.

Put the mint, poppy and sesame seeds on to different plates and roll the lamb balls in the mint, the beef in the poppy seeds and the pork in the sesame seeds. Thread each type of meatball on to different thin skewers, pressing them on well.

Cook on the greased grill of a barbecue, putting the pork on first as it needs 10-12 minutes, then the lamb (8-10 minutes), and lastly the beef (only 6-8 minutes). Turn the skewers during cooking, then serve very hot with a variety of dips.

■ COOK'S TIP

Five spice powder is an aromatic seasoning made up of star anise, fennel, cloves, cinnamon and Szechuan pepper. It makes these ribs aromatic and oriental, though it's not an essential ingredient. Look for it in Chinese shops and supermarkets.

■ COOK'S TIP

A chilli dip, such as Mexican chilli sauce (recipe 199), would go well here. Use fresh sesame and poppy seeds; old stock will lack crispness and taste.

35 NUT-STUFFED PEACHES

Preparation time:
10 minutes

Serves 4

Calories:
292 per portion

YOU WILL NEED:
4 ripe peaches, peeled, halved and
  stoned
2 tablespoons lemon juice
225 g/8 oz cottage cheese
100 g/4 oz pecan nuts, finely
  chopped
8 lettuce leaves

Put the peaches in a mixing bowl and sprinkle with the lemon juice. Toss so that they become well coated in the juice.

Mix together the cottage cheese and pecan nuts.

Arrange the lettuce leaves on four individual serving dishes. Place two peach halves on each dish, cut sides up. Spoon the cottage cheese mixture into the centres and serve.

36 CRABMEAT STARTER

Preparation time:
10 minutes

Serves 4

Calories:
842 per portion

YOU WILL NEED:
450 g/1 lb cooked crabmeat
1 large Webb lettuce, separated
  into leaves
4 firm tomatoes, skinned and sliced
1 avocado, peeled, stoned, sliced
  and gently rubbed with lemon
  juice
½ cucumber, thinly sliced
9 black olives, stoned
FOR THE REMOULADE SAUCE
300 ml/½ pint mayonnaise
1 teaspoon anchovy essence
½ teaspoon finely chopped fresh
parsley
1½ teaspoons capers (optional)
1 hard-boiled egg, chopped
1 garlic clove, crushed
1 teaspoon finely chopped fresh
  tarragon

Mix together the ingredients for the rémoulade sauce.

Remove any shell and cartilage from the crabmeat and flake the fish.

Arrange the lettuce leaves on a large serving dish. Put the crabmeat in the centre of the dish and arrange the tomatoes, avocado, cucumber and olives around the crabmeat. Pour over the sauce and serve at once.

■ COOK'S TIP

Pecan nuts are used in sweet and savoury dishes. They are related to the walnut, which would make an acceptable substitute in this recipe.

■ COOK'S TIP

Ready-prepared crabmeat from the fishmonger is ideal for this salad-style starter. You could also buy a cooked crab and shell it, removing the meat yourself.

FISH & SHELLFISH

Fish and shellfish are perfect summer foods. Light and delicately flavoured, they fit into all kinds of warm-weather menus. Fish is easily cooked on a barbecue; use a grill rack with a handle to prevent the delicate flesh breaking up and do not overcook it. Fish on skewers cooks over barbecue coals wonderfully quickly, too.

37 ITALIAN FISH BAKE

Preparation time:	YOU WILL NEED:
15 minutes	*4 x 225-275 g/8-10 oz red mullet*
	salt and pepper
Cooking time:	*1 small sweet red pepper, seeded*
about 30 minutes	*1 small sweet green pepper, seeded*
	350 g/12 oz courgettes, trimmed
Serves 4	*1 medium-sized onion, sliced*
	100 g/4 oz button mushrooms,
Calories:	* sliced*
531 per portion	*1 garlic clove, finely chopped*
	25 g/1 oz butter or margarine

Clean the fish (or ask the fishmonger to do it for you). Trim off the fins, then wash and dry.

Have ready 4 sheets of foil, each large enough to enclose a fish plus vegetables, and grease lightly. Lay a fish on each sheet and season with salt and pepper to taste. Slice the pepper flesh, and thinly slice the courgettes. Arrange all the vegetables and garlic around the fish and dot with the butter.

Fold up the foil to make airtight parcels and arrange on the barbecue grid. Barbecue for about 30 minutes, or until the fish and vegetables are cooked. Accompany with a new potato salad.

38 SMOKED SALMON ROLLS

Preparation time:	YOU WILL NEED:
40 minutes, plus	*1 small smoked trout about 350-*
chilling	* 400 g/12-14 oz, skinned and*
	* filleted into 4 long pieces*
Serves 6	*6 tablespoons double cream*
	4 tablespoons soured cream
Calories:	*1½ tablespoons creamed*
339 per portion	* horseradish*
	¼ teaspoon cayenne pepper
	12 thin slices smoked salmon,
	* about 425 g/15 oz total weight*
	50 g/2 oz red caviar or red
	* lumpfish roe*
	freshly ground black pepper
	12 thin slices of lemon
	parsley sprigs, to garnish

Cut each fillet of smoked trout into 3 pieces and reserve. Beat the double cream until it forms soft peaks, then fold in the soured cream and creamed horseradish. Season with the cayenne pepper and then spread each slice of smoked salmon with a little of the mixture.

Put a small piece of caviar or lumpfish roe at one end of each slice, spreading it slightly then sprinkle with pepper. Place a piece of smoked trout on top of the caviar, then carefully roll up the salmon slice, starting at the smoked trout end.

Arrange the rolls on a platter, with a slice of lemon between each roll, garnish with parsley and chill for at least 1 hour. Serve chilled with lightly buttered brown bread.

■ COOK'S TIP

This recipe is also good for grey mullet, snapper, trout or cod steaks.

■ COOK'S TIP

Red caviar is strictly not caviar at all since it comes from the dog salmon, native to the Siberian rivers running into the Pacific, and off the west Canadian coast. The taste is similar but more salty than the true caviar. Red lumpfish roe makes an excellent substitute.

39 DEEP SEA SKEWERS

Preparation time:
20 minutes, plus
marinating

Cooking time:
10 minutes

Serves 4

Calories:
241 per portion

YOU WILL NEED:
4 streaky bacon rashers, rinded
2 cod or halibut steaks, skinned
    and quartered
salt and pepper
8 large cooked prawns, peeled
4 mushrooms
4 tomatoes, halved
watercress sprigs, to garnish
FOR THE MARINADE
6 tablespoons lemon juice
large pinch of paprika
2 tablespoons vegetable oil
1 bay leaf
1 parsley sprig
1 small onion, sliced

To make the marinade, combine all the ingredients with salt
and pepper to taste in a large shallow bowl.

Stretch the bacon rashers with the back of a knife, then cut
in half crossways. Season the fish pieces, then roll each piece in
a piece of bacon and place in the marinade. Add the prawns
and mushrooms and turn to coat. Cover and leave to marinate
in the refrigerator, turning occasionally, for 4 hours.

Drain, reserving the marinade. Thread fish rolls, prawns
and mushrooms on to 4 oiled kebab skewers with the halved
tomatoes, alternating the ingredients. Brush well with the
reserved marinade. Cook on a hot barbecue, turning from time
to time, and basting with marinade, for about 10 minutes or
until tender. Serve garnished with watercress sprigs.

■ COOK'S TIP

*For a special occasion, use 8
-10 large scallops instead of
the fish steaks. Wrapped in
bacon, they will take a little
less time than the halibut to
cook.*

40 MARINATED KIPPER FILLETS WITH SOURED CREAM SAUCE

Preparation time:
15 minutes, plus
marinating

Serves 6

Calories:
242 per portion

YOU WILL NEED:
1 tablespoon lemon juice
1 teaspoon salt
1 tablespoon sugar
1 teaspoon coarsely ground black
    peppercorns
1 tablespoon chopped fresh dill
1 tablespoon brandy
3 kipper fillets, each 150 g/5 oz,
    cut in half lengthways to
    make 6 pieces and skinned
FOR THE SAUCE
150 ml/¼ pint soured cream
5 tablespoons chopped fresh dill
freshly ground white pepper

Mix together the lemon juice, salt, sugar, peppercorns, dill and
brandy and sprinkle a quarter of the mixture over a shallow
dish. Lay 3 of the fillets, skinned side down, in the dish and
rub most of the remaining mixture into them. Cover with the
other 3 fillets, skinned side up, and sprinkle over the remaining
marinade. Cover with greaseproof paper, then foil, and weight
the fish down with 2 heavy cans. Chill for at least 12 hours.

To make the sauce, whisk together the soured cream, fresh
dill and a generous sprinkling of ground white pepper and put
into a serving bowl and chill.

To serve, arrange the fillets on a platter, garnish with
lemon wedges and serve with the soured cream sauce.

■ COOK'S TIP

*Kippers make an unusual
and exotic dish treated in
this way. A tail piece of
salmon can also be used for
this recipe. Both kippers
and salmon could be*

*prepared up to 3 days in
advance and kept chilled.*

41   HERRINGS WITH HOT PEPPER SAUCE

Preparation time:	YOU WILL NEED:
15 minutes, plus marinating and chilling	2 large red peppers
	100 ml/3½ fl oz olive oil, plus 2 tablespoons
	1 anchovy fillet, pounded
Cooking time:	5 tablespoons lemon juice
15 minutes	salt and pepper
	few drops Tabasco sauce
Serves 6	6 herrings, filleted

Calories:
356 per portion

Cut the peppers in half and remove the seeds. Cook, cut side down, under a hot grill for 3-4 minutes until the skin blackens and blisters. Cool for a few minutes, then peel off the skin. Chop the peppers roughly, put in a bowl, cover with the 100 ml/3½ fl oz oil, and leave, covered, in a cool place for 2 hours.

Put the peppers and oil into a liquidizer and blend to a purée. Add the anchovy fillet and 3 tablespoons of the lemon juice and blend again. Transfer to a bowl, add a few drops of Tabasco to taste. Chill until required.

Brush the herrings on both sides with the remaining oil and then the remaining lemon juice. Sprinkle with salt and freshly ground black pepper and cook on the greased grill of a preheated barbecue, skin side up, for 5-6 minutes. Turn the herrings over and cook for 3-4 minutes until crisp. Serve sizzling hot with the pepper sauce handed round separately.

■ COOK'S TIP

The piquancy of this sauce perfectly complements the rich flavour of the herrings. If preferred, leave the peppers chopped and serve as a salad with the fish.

42   ITALIAN FISH SALAD

Preparation time:	YOU WILL NEED:
45 minutes	225 g/8 oz pasta short-cut shapes
Cooking time:	450 g/1 lb squid, cleaned
25 minutes	5 tablespoons olive oil
Serves 6	3 garlic cloves, crushed
Calories:	1 kg/2 lb fresh mussels, cleaned
519 per portion	100 g/4 oz peeled prawns
	salt and pepper
	6 sticks celery, sliced, tops reserved
	1 green and 1 red pepper, cored, seeded and cut into strips
	FOR THE DRESSING
	8 tablespoons olive oil
	2 tablespoons lemon juice
	2 teaspoons finely chopped parsley
	unshelled prawns, to garnish

Cook the pasta in salted boiling water for 12-15 minutes until just tender. Drain. Rinse with cold water and drain thoroughly.

Cut the squid body into rings. Reserve the tentacles. Rinse and dry. Sit a frying pan over high heat and cook the squid rings, stirring, for 3-4 minutes. Wipe the pan, heat 1 tablespoon of the oil and lightly fry one garlic clove. Return the squid and tentacles to the pan, cook 3 minutes, then transfer to a bowl.

Place the frying pan over high heat again, then add the mussels with another garlic clove. Cover and cook, shaking the pan, for 5 minutes or until the mussels have opened. Discard any which do not open. Mix the squid, shelled mussels and peeled prawns together and season lightly. Mix together the remaining garlic, dressing ingredients and seasoning and pour over the fish. Add the celery, peppers and pasta and toss well.

■ COOK'S TIP

To clean squid, take hold of the head and tentacles and pull them cleanly away from the body. Thoroughly rinse the body pouch, removing the transparent spine, then peel off the skin. Cut off and discard the head and innards and wash the tentacles thoroughly.

43 SMOKY CHILLED PRAWNS

Preparation time:
25 minutes, plus
marinating

Cooking time:
6 minutes

Serves 4

Calories:
244 per portion

YOU WILL NEED:
10 small green chillies
20 cooked jumbo prawns, peeled
5 tablespoons olive oil
coarsely ground sea salt
lemon wedges

Cut the stems off the chillies, then slit the chillies in half and carefully remove the seeds. Avoid rubbing your eyes with hands that have touched the chilli as this will burn.

Wrap one half of each chilli round the middle of a jumbo prawn and thread 5 on to a skewer.

Place the skewers in a long shallow dish and cover with the oil and the salt. Leave, covered, in a cool place for 30 minutes, covered.

Cook the prawns on the greased grill of a preheated barbecue for 3 minutes each side, basting with any left-over marinade.

Serve hot with lemon wedges.

44 SARDINES IN VINE LEAVES

Preparation time:
30 minutes, plus
marinating

Cooking time:
6-8 minutes

Serves 4-6

Calories:
813 - 542 per
portion

YOU WILL NEED:
24 small sardines, about 1.5 kg/3 lb,
*   defrosted if frozen*
175 ml/6 fl oz olive oil
4 tablespoons lemon juice
3 garlic cloves, finely chopped
6 sprigs fresh thyme, finely chopped
2 shallots, peeled and chopped
½ teaspoon dried oregano
salt and pepper
24 prepared large vine leaves

Rinse the sardines carefully in cold water, then pat dry.

Put the sardines in a shallow dish, then pour over the oil, lemon juice and add the garlic, thyme, shallots and dried oregano. Cover and leave in a cool place for 1 hour.

Remove the sardines from the marinade, reserving the latter. If there are any pieces of garlic, onion or herb clinging to the fish, leave them on. Sprinkle them with salt and black pepper.

Place the prepared vine leaves on a flat surface, and brush the vein side with a little of the marinade.

Roll up each sardine in a vine leaf, placing the sardine head at the stem end. Press the leaves gently to seal the package. The head and tails may protrude slightly at each end but this does not matter. Brush the vine leaves with a little more of the marinade. Cook the sardines in a hinged grill on a preheated barbecue for 3-4 minutes each side, basting with any leftover marinade, until the vine leaves are crispy.

▓ COOK'S TIP

Jumbo prawns are sometimes called king size prawns – they are the large Mediterranean prawns which are half the size of crayfish. The other essential ingredient here is an aromatic branch or two of myrtle, juniper, rosemary or fennel to get that smoky flavour from the barbecue.

▓ COOK'S TIP

If using fresh vine leaves, wash thoroughly in hot water then blanch over medium heat for 20-30 minutes. Rinse in cold water and dry.

45 RED TROUT WITH FENNEL MAYONNAISE

Preparation time: 25 minutes	YOU WILL NEED: 1-2 teaspoons tarragon vinegar 300 ml/½ pint mayonnaise (see Cook's Tip)
Cooking time: 15 minutes	1 small bulb fresh fennel freshly ground black pepper
Serves 4	175 g/6 oz butter, softened 1 teaspoon lemon juice
Calories: 1039 per portion	4 red (pink) trout, 225 g/8 oz cleaned weight, heads and tails left on dried fennel stalks, for cooking

Whisk ½ teaspoon tarragon vinegar into the mayonnaise, then whisk in another ½ teaspoon. If necessary, gradually add up to another teaspoon vinegar. The flavour should not be too sharp.

Trim the hard stalks and feathery leaves from the fennel bulb. Finely chop the feathery leaves and reserve. Finely slice or grate the fennel bulb, then fold into the mayonnaise. Season with black pepper, cover with cling film and chill.

Mash together the butter, lemon juice and some pepper. Pat the fish dry, then put 1 teaspoon of the butter inside each fish and close the cavity, fixing with a toothpick. Spread each fish with the remaining butter and place in a hinged grill.

Douse the dried fennel stalks with cold water, then place on the barbecue coals. Cook the fish on the barbecue for 7 minutes on each side. Serve with the mayonnaise handed round separately. Garnish the fish with the lemon wedges.

46 SPICY COD STEAKS IN FOIL

Preparation time: 15 minutes	YOU WILL NEED: 4 cod steaks, about 225 g/8 oz each 6 tablespoons olive oil
Cooking time: 20 minutes	1 medium onion, finely sliced into rings
Serves 4	2 medium tomatoes, finely sliced 2 tablespoons finely chopped fresh coriander
Calories: 313 per portion	½ teaspoon medium hot curry powder 2 tablespoons lemon juice salt and pepper coriander sprigs, to garnish

Cut out 4 large squares of heavy duty foil and grease lightly with a little oil, then place 1 cod steak in the centre of each piece of foil.

Put a few onion rings on top of each steak, then a few tomato slices on top of the onions.

Sprinkle with coriander leaves, then mix together the remaining oil, curry powder and lemon juice and pour some over each steak. Season with salt and pepper, then fold the foil over and seal the packages.

Put the packages on the coals of a preheated barbecue and cook for 20 minutes.

Remove the packages and serve, garnished with coriander sprigs.

■ COOK'S TIP

Make the mayonnaise with 3 egg yolks, pinch of sea salt and 300 ml/½ pint room temperature olive oil. At first, whisk the oil into the beaten egg yolks and *salt drop by drop. When a third of the oil has been used, start adding it in a thin, steady stream. A thick, yellow consistency should be the result.*

■ COOK'S TIP

The cod steaks can be served hot, straight from the barbecue or, which is just as delicious, let them cool in their packages and then serve them cold.

47 BARBECUED LOBSTER

Preparation time:	YOU WILL NEED:
15 minutes	1 freshly boiled lobster, about
	750 g/1½ lb
Cooking time:	50 g/2 oz butter
20-25 minutes	2 tablespoons brandy
	4 tablespoons double cream
Serves 2	salt and pepper
	shredded lettuce
Calories:	
292 per portion	

Crack the large claws of the lobster with a quick, sharp blow from a heavy knife, and then slightly loosen the body and tail meat. Do not take the meat right out but lift the edges a little so that the butter mixture can seep down the sides.

Put the butter, brandy and cream in a small pan and heat over the barbecue until the butter has melted and is bubbling, whisking constantly. Keep the pan on the side of the barbecue.

Brush the lobster flesh all over with some of the mixture and then cook the lobster halves, shell sides down, over the barbecue for 15-20 minutes, basting every 2 minutes, until the flesh feels warm to the touch.

Baste again, then turn the lobster halves over carefully and cook for a further 3 minutes, just to brown the tops.

Put the pan containing the butter and cream mixture back over the coals and heat until bubbling. Place the lobsters on a bed of shredded lettuce and pour over the remaining mixture.

Season with freshly ground black pepper and serve hot.

48 PEPPERED MONKFISH KEBABS

Preparation time:	YOU WILL NEED:
10 minutes, plus	500 g/ ¼ lb monkfish, cut into
marinating	2.5 cm/1 inch cubes
	150 ml/5 fl oz natural yogurt
Cooking time:	1 tablespoon black peppercorns,
10-15 minutes	lightly crushed
	3 tablespoons olive oil
Serves 4-6	salt
	lemon slices, to garnish
Calories:	
149 - 99 per portion	

Put the monkfish cubes in a large bowl, add the yogurt, peppercorns, oil and a generous sprinkling of salt. Stir everything together then leave, covered, in a cool place for 1 hour to marinate.

Thread the fish on to long skewers, and cook on the greased grill of a preheated barbecue for 10-15 minutes, turning and basting with the marinade every 2-3 minutes. Serve garnished with the lemon slices.

■ COOK'S TIP

To prepare a lobster, lie it on its back then split it down the middle with a cleaver. The stomach sac is a little bag near the head and comes out easily.

Discard it, then pull out the long black vein running along the body. Other parts not eaten are the feathery gills between the head meat and the small legs.

■ COOK'S TIP

The monkfish and its marinade may be prepared up to 24 hours in advance and kept in the fridge. Stand at room temperature before cooking.

49 MARINATED BABY SOLES

Preparation time:
5 minutes, plus
marinating

Cooking time:
10 minutes

Serves 6

Calories:
209 per portion

YOU WILL NEED:
6 Dover soles, about 225 g/8 oz
   each, dark skin removed
150 ml/¼ pint fresh lime juice
150 ml/¼ pint dry white wine
1 tablespoon clear honey
3 tablespoons peanut oil
pinch of ground allspice
2 teaspoons soy sauce
salt and pepper
FOR THE GARNISH
lime wedges
coriander sprigs

Lay the sole in a shallow dish. Combine all the remaining ingredients, except the lime wedges, and coriander sprigs, and pour over the fish. Cover and leave to marinate for 3 hours, turning 2-3 times.

Remove the fish from the marinade and cook on the greased grill of a preheated barbecue for 5 minutes each side, constantly basting with the marinade. Serve very hot, garnished with lime wedges and coriander sprigs.

50 PRAWN AND TURKEY KEBABS

Preparation time:
15 minutes, plus
marinating

Cooking time:
10-15 minutes

Serves 4

Calories:
189 per portion

YOU WILL NEED:
2 portions turkey breast, skinned,
   boned and cut into squares
1 small red pepper, cored, seeded
   and cut into squares
1 small green pepper, cored,
   seeded and cut into squares
100-250 g/4-8 oz large prawns,
   peeled
Soured cream marinade
   (recipe 197)

Put the turkey, red and green peppers and prawns in a shallow dish. Pour over the marinade and turn to coat the ingredients. Leave to marinate for at least 1 hour.

Thread the turkey, peppers and prawns alternatively on to skewers. Brush well with the marinade and cook over a medium-hot barbecue fire, turning and basting with the marinade from time to time.

■ COOK'S TIP

The same recipe can be used for small whole plaice or lemon sole, or for plaice fillets which should be rolled after marinating and put on skewers.

■ COOK'S TIP

Serve these kebabs on a bed of Pilaff rice (recipe 142) and with a crisp green salad.

 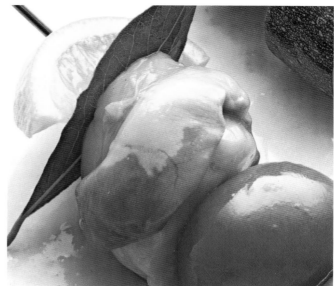

51 BARBECUED TROUT

Preparation time:
10 minutes, plus marinating

Cooking time:
15-20 minutes

Serves 4

Calories:
356 per portion

YOU WILL NEED:
50 g/2 oz butter, melted
2 tablespoons lemon juice
2 tablespoons chopped fresh parsley
salt and pepper
4 trout, cleaned and washed

Mix together the butter, lemon juice, parsley and salt and pepper to taste. Brush the trout inside and out with the butter mixture. Cook on the grid on the barbecue, turning several times and brushing with the lemon butter towards the end of the cooking time.

52 BARBECUED SCALLOPS

Preparation time:
10 minutes, plus marinating

Cooking time:
5-6 minutes

Serves 4

Calories:
199 per portion

YOU WILL NEED:
8-12 scallops
4 tomatoes
4 bay leaves (optional)
25 g/1 oz butter, melted
FOR THE MARINADE
150 ml/¼ pint white wine
2 tablespoons lemon juice
1 onion, sliced
1 carrot, sliced
1 celery stalk, chopped
1 fresh parsley sprig, or
  ½ teaspoon dried parsley
1 fresh thyme sprig or
  ½ teaspoon dried thyme
1 bay leaf
6 black peppercorns, slightly
  crushed
2-4 tablespoons oil

First, make the marinade. Mix all the ingredients together and allow to stand for about 1 hour before using.

Place the scallops in the marinade and leave to marinate for 2 - 3 hours in the refrigerator. Thread the scallops on to skewers alternately with whole tomatoes and bay leaves, if used. Brush with the melted butter and cook on the barbecue grid, turning and basting with the marinade from time to time.

■ COOK'S TIP

Fish for barbecue cooking should be fresh and firm. A grill rack with a handle is ideal for barbecuing fish: the fish can be turned easily and will not break up.

■ COOK'S TIP

This white wine marinade is very good with veal, pork, poultry and fish. Replace the white wine with red for a marinade for red meat or turkey.

53   SCAMPI KEBABS

Preparation time:	YOU WILL NEED:
10 minutes, plus	*16 Dublin Bay prawns, peeled*
marinating	*2 green peppers, cored, seeded and*
	cut into 16 pieces
Cooking time:	*16 medium mushrooms*
10 minutes	*16 sage leaves*
	2 lemons, quartered, then cut in half
Serves 4	FOR THE MARINADE
	4 tablespoons olive oil
Calories:	*1 tablespoons lemon juice*
438 per portion	*1-2 garlic cloves, crushed*
	1 teaspoon salt
	½ teaspoon freshly ground black
	pepper

Mix together the marinade ingredients in a large, shallow mixing bowl. Add the prawns and stir well. Leave in the refrigerator to marinate for up to 1 hour.

Remove the prawns from the marinade and pat dry with absorbent kitchen paper. Reserve any remaining marinade. Thread 1 prawn on to a kebab skewer, then a piece of green pepper, a mushroom, sage leaf and lemon segment. Repeat the process 3 more times to the end of the skewer. Repeat with three more skewers. Place on the rack in the grill pan, baste with the marinade and grill for 10 minutes, turning occasionally and basting from time to time.

Remove from the heat and transfer to a warmed serving dish. Pour over the pan juices and serve.

54   SALMON WITH DILL

Preparation time:	YOU WILL NEED:
5 minutes, plus	*4 salmon steaks*
marinating	*4 tablespoons sunflower oil*
	6 sprigs fresh dill (or 1 teaspoon
Cooking time:	*dried)*
about 12 minutes	*salt and pepper*
	1 lemon
Serves 4	*½ cucumber, sliced*
Calories:	
302 per portion	

Lay the salmon steaks in a shallow dish, pour over the oil. Top with dill and sprinkle with salt and pepper. Cut the lemon in half. Squeeze the juice from one half over the salmon. Cut the other half into 4 thick slices, reserving them for garnish.

Marinate the salmon for 30 minutes, then grill over medium hot coals for about 6 minutes on each side, turning and brushing with the marinade occasionally. Take care not to overcook the salmon, or it will begin to break up. When the flesh has turned pink and is firm, it will be cooked. Serve on a bed of sliced cucumber with the lemon slices.

▧ COOK'S TIP

If Dublin Bay prawns (scampi or langoustine) are not available, use any large prawn or monkfish cubes in this recipe.

▧ COOK'S TIP

Deliciously simple! Cook the salmon steaks on foil if they are thin, or they may fall apart.

55 ORIENTAL FISH

Preparation time:
10 minutes, plus marinating

Cooking time:
8-10 minutes

Serves 4

Calories:
166 per portion

YOU WILL NEED:
6 tablespoons soy sauce
1 garlic clove, crushed
2 tablespoons sesame oil
2 tablespoons brown sugar
2 tablespoons lemon juice
pinch of ginger
4 small plaice, sole or dabs
1 spring onion, chopped

Mix the soy sauce, garlic, oil, sugar, lemon juice and ginger together and pour into a shallow dish. Lay the fish on top, turn them in the marinade to coat and leave for 1 hour.

Cover the grill with greased foil and place the fish on top. Grill over hot coals for 4-5 minutes on each side. Sprinkle with spring onion and serve.

COOK'S TIP

This Japanese-style marinade is delicious brushed over any white fish fillets, small whole fish or kebabs.

56 BACON-SCALLOP SKEWERS

Preparation time:
10 minutes

Cooking time:
5 minutes

Serves 8

Calories:
159 per portion

YOU WILL NEED:
8 scallops
8 rashers streaky bacon
juice of 1 lemon
50 g/2 oz butter, melted
1 tablespoon chopped fresh parsley

Cut the scallops and bacon rashers in half. Roll up each piece of bacon. Thread scallops and bacon rolls alternately on to metal skewers. Sprinkle each with lemon juice and brush with butter. Grill over hot coals for 5 minutes, turning and basting frequently with butter.

Sprinkle the cooked scallops with parsley and serve with brown bread and butter.

COOK'S TIP

Scallops and bacon are always favourites. Prepare them in advance; cover, and then they take just 5 minutes to cook.

57 SMOKED FISHCAKES

Preparation time:
15 minutes, plus
chilling

Cooking time:
about 20 minutes

Makes 10

Calories:
72 per fishcake

YOU WILL NEED:
*1 x 350-g/12-oz packet frozen
    boil-in-the-bag smoked haddock
350 g/12 oz cold cooked mashed
    potato
2 tablespoons chopped fresh
    coriander or parsley
pinch of paprika
salt and pepper
beaten egg, to bind
oil*

Cook the haddock as directed on the packet. Drain and flake
the flesh; add to the mashed potato with the coriander or
parsley, paprika and salt and black pepper. Mash well together
with a fork, adding enough egg to bind the mixture to a firm
paste.

Using floured hands shape the mixture into ten flat neat fish
cakes about 8 cm/2½ in round. Place on a floured tray and chill
for 30 minutes.

Cover the grill-rack with foil. Brush the fish cakes with a
little oil and grill over medium-hot coals for 5-8 minutes on
each side, carefully using a fish slice to turn them over.

Serve the fishcakes hot, with slices of lemon and sprigs of
parsley.

58 FISH PARCELS

Preparation time:
15 minutes

Cooking time:
20-30 minutes

Serves 4

Calories:
148 per portion

YOU WILL NEED:
*4 cod or haddock steaks
salt and pepper
4 button mushrooms
½ small onion
4 tomatoes
25 g/1 oz peas
25 g/1 oz butter
1 tablespoon lemon juice*

Place each fish steak on a square of foil. Sprinkle with salt and
pepper. Slice the mushrooms; peel and very finely chop the
onion; chop the tomatoes. Divide the mushrooms, onion, tomato
and peas over the fish steaks. Dot with butter and sprinkle with
lemon juice. Wrap the foil loosely around the fish, making sure
the folds are tightly sealed. Place over hot coals and cook for
20-30 minutes. Serve sprinkled with chopped parsley.

▪ COOK'S TIP

*Use boil-in-the-bag
haddock for speed, or
poach fresh smoked fish in
milk, using the milk later to
make a white sauce.*

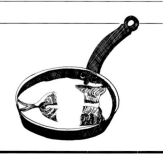

▪ COOK'S TIP

*Buy either fresh fillets or
frozen steaks for this recipe,
which is almost a complete
meal.*

59 GRILLED MARINATED SARDINES

Preparation time:	YOU WILL NEED:
10 minutes, plus marinating	12 fresh sardines, cleaned
	FOR THE MARINADE
	2 tablespoons lemon juice
Cooking time:	3 tablespoons cider vinegar
8-10 minutes	1 tablespoon clear honey
	1 tablespoon oil
Serves 4	150 ml/¼ pint dry cider

Calories:
674 per portion

Place the sardines in a shallow dish. Make the marinade by beating the lemon juice with the vinegar, honey, oil and cider, blending well. Pour over the sardines, cover and leave to marinate in the refrigerator for 2-3 hours, turning occasionally.

Remove the sardines with a slotted spoon and place directly on the grill, or in a grill rack, and cook over hot coals for 8-10 minutes, turning once. Baste from time to time with the marinade.

Serve hot with chive butter (see Cook's Tip) and a dish of Ratatouille (see recipe 160).

60 TUNA STEAKS WITH MUSTARD

Preparation time:	YOU WILL NEED:
15 minutes	50 g/2 oz butter, melted
	3 teaspoons made mustard
Cooking time:	1 tablespoon lemon juice
20 minutes	salt and pepper
	4 individual tuna or cod steaks
Serves 4	lemon slices, to garnish

Calories:
207 per portion

Combine the melted butter with the mustard, lemon juice and seasoning to taste. Brush half this mixture over the steaks, on both sides, then grill over medium coals for 10 minutes. Turn, brush with the remaining mixture and grill for a further 10 minutes.

Serve hot, with any of the remaining mustard mixture and lemon slices to garnish. Ratatouille (see recipe 160) would go well with this.

COOK'S TIP

For chive butter, excellent with barbecued fish, beat together 50 g/2 oz butter, 2 teaspoons snipped fresh chives, 1 teaspoon lemon juice, salt and pepper.

COOK'S TIP

Both the hot yellow English-style mustard and the sweeter Dijon mustard would go well in this recipe.

61 SKEWERED PLAICE

Preparation time:
15 minutes, plus
marinating

Cooking time:
10 minutes

Serves 4

Calories:
373 per portion

YOU WILL NEED:
12 rashers streaky bacon
450 g/1 lb plaice fillets
FOR THE MARINADE
2 tablespoons soy sauce
3 tablespoons cider vinegar
1 tablespoon clear honey
1 tablespoon safflower oil
150 ml/¼ pint dry still cider

First, make the marinade: blend the ingredients for the marinade together thoroughly.

Place the bacon rashers on a board and stretch with the back of a round-bladed knife. Cut each rasher in half. Remove the skin from the plaice fillets and divide into 24 pieces. Place each on a halved rasher of bacon and roll up. Secure with a wooden cocktail stick. Place in a dish with the marinade and leave to marinate for 2 hours.

Remove the rolls from the marinade, remove the cocktail sticks and place on four skewers. Grill on the barbecue, over medium coals, for 8-10 minutes, turning and brushing from time to time with the marinade. Serve hot with lemon wedges and crusty bread.

62 BARBECUED MACKEREL WITH DILL

Preparation time:
15 minutes

Cooking time:
20 minutes

Serves 4

Calories:
472 per portion

YOU WILL NEED:
4 medium mackerel
2 tablespoons salad oil
juice of 1 lemon
salt and black pepper
sprigs of dill
Gooseberry herb sauce
(see Cook's Tip)

Clean the mackerel, removing the heads if desired. Slash the flesh diagonally on each side of the fish about three times. Brush with the oil and lemon juice. Season to taste and scatter with the sprigs of dill.

Grill over medium coals for 10 minutes on each side, turning once and brushing from time to time with the oil and lemon juice. Serve with Gooseberry herb sauce.

■ COOK'S TIP

This marinade would also work well with cubes of white fish, such as cod, haddock or monkfish.

■ COOK'S TIP

For Gooseberry herb sauce, simmer together for 10 minutes 225 g/8 oz gooseberries (topped and tailed), 4½ tablespoons water, 2 tablespoons caster sugar, 25 g/1 oz butter, 1 tablespoon each chopped fennel and parsley.

63 OTAK OTAK

Preparation time:	YOU WILL NEED:
20 minutes, plus	*coconut milk (see Cook's Tip)*
cooling	*6-8 dried red chillies, crushed*
	1 medium-sized onion, very finely
Cooking time:	*chopped*
about 20 minutes	*50 g/2 oz roast salted peanuts,*
	very finely chopped
Serves 8	*finely grated rind of ½ lemon*
	8 basil leaves, chopped
Calories:	*1 egg, beaten*
214 per portion	*½ teaspoon ground turmeric*
	salt and pepper
	8 x 175-g/6-oz cod steaks
	sprigs of coriander or parsley, to
	garnish

First make the coconut milk (see Cook's Tip).

Mix together the crushed chillies, onion, peanuts, lemon rind and basil in a bowl. Stir in the coconut milk, egg and turmeric and season with salt and pepper to taste.

Have ready 8 sheets of foil, each large enough to enclose a fish steak loosely. Place a cod steak on each sheet and spoon the chilli mixture on top. Fold up the foil and crimp the edges together to make the airtight parcels.

Arrange the foil parcels on the barbecue grid. Barbecue for about 20 minutes, or until the fish flakes easily when tested with a fork. Transfer the steaks and topping to a serving dish and garnish with herbs. Hand lemon wedges separately.

■ COOK'S TIP

For coconut milk, put 50 g/ 2 oz desiccated coconut in a bowl and pour over 150 ml/¼ pint boiling water. Set aside to cool, then strain, pressing the coconut to extract as much liquid as possible. Keep the 'milk' and discard the coconut.

64 BARBECUED FISH KEBABS

Preparation time:	YOU WILL NEED:
20 minutes	*4 whole mackerel or herring,*
	cleaned
Cooking time:	*3 small onions, quartered*
10 minutes	*4 tomatoes, halved*
	FOR THE SAUCE
Serves 4	*300 ml/½ pint chicken or fish*
	stock
Calories:	*150 ml/¼ pint tomato ketchup*
423 per portion	*2 tablespoons Worcestershire*
	sauce
	2 tablespoons wine vinegar
	2 tablespoons brown sugar
	2 drops of Tabasco sauce
	2 tablespoons tomato purée
	1 tablespoon cornflour
	salt and pepper

Trim the fish then open out on a board with the skin side upwards and press along the backbones. Remove the bones. Reshape the fish and cut each across into 4 pieces.

For the sauce, mix together all the ingredients, except the seasoning, in a pan and stir until boiling. Add salt and pepper to taste. Keep the sauce warm in the pan on the side of the barbecue.

Thread the fish on 4 oiled skewers alternating with pieces of onion and tomato halves. Place on the greased grid. Barbecue for 10 minutes, turning the skewers frequently and brushing them with a little of the sauce during cooking.

■ COOK'S TIP

For a complete meal serve the kebabs on a bed of rice, with the sauce served separately.

65   MUSTARDY MACKEREL

Preparation time:
10 minutes

Cooking time:
about 20 minutes

Serves 4

Calories:
585 per portion

YOU WILL NEED:

1 x 425 g/15 oz can borlotti beans,
drained

3 tablespoons bottled American
style mild mustard sauce

4 spring onions, trimmed and
chopped

4 tablespoons finely chopped
mixed herbs

sea salt and pepper

4 medium-sized mackerel, cleaned

4 sticks of celery, thinly sliced

4 tablespoons vinaigrette dressing

2 tomatoes, halved, to garnish

Rinse the beans with cold water if necessary and drain again. Take 4 tablespoons of the beans and mix with half the sauce, the onion and herbs. Season with salt and pepper to taste and use to stuff the mackerel.

Brush the stuffed fish with half the remaining sauce and arrange in a foil grill tray. Barbecue for about 10 minutes then turn the fish carefully. Brush with the remaining sauce and continue cooking for a further 10 minutes, or until the flesh flakes easily when tested with a fork. Garnish with the tomato halves.

Combine the remaining beans with the celery and vinaigrette and serve with the fish.

66   SALMON STEAKS WITH BASIL AND LEMON BUTTER

Preparation time:
15 minutes, plus
chilling

Cooking time:
9 minutes

Serves 4

Calories:
357 per portion

YOU WILL NEED:

1 lemon

1 tablespoon chopped basil or 1
teaspoon dried basil

50 g/2 oz butter, softened

salt and pepper

4 x 175-g/6-oz salmon steaks

little oil

Pare a few fine strips of lemon rind and cut into shreds. Finely grate the remaining lemon rind and squeeze the juice. Beat the basil, lemon juice and grated rind into the butter and season with salt and pepper to taste. Place on a sheet of foil and gather the herb butter into a ball. Chill well.

Brush the salmon steaks with oil and place on the greased grid. Barbecue for 5 minutes, turn the steaks carefully and cook for a further 4 minutes. Place a quarter of the herb butter on each steak, top with shreds of lemon rind and serve.

■ COOK'S TIP

Try this recipe with herrings instead of mackerel.

■ COOK'S TIP

For salmon with orange and tarragon butter, substitute 1 orange for the lemon and use tarragon instead of the basil. Pour half the orange juice over *the salmon steaks in a dish and leave to stand for 1 hour before cooking. Make the herb butter with the remaining orange juice.*

67 BEACH BARBECUED RED MULLET

Preparation time:	YOU WILL NEED:
10 minutes	*4 x 225-275 g/8-10 oz red mullet, cleaned*
Cooking time:	*salt and pepper*
16 minutes	*1 small onion, sliced*
	4 sprigs of thyme
Serves 4	*2 tablespoons lemon juice*
	50 g/2 oz butter, melted

Calories:
561 per portion

Wash the mullet and dry inside and out with absorbent kitchen paper. Sprinkle the cavities with salt and pepper to taste, add a few onion slices and a sprig of thyme to each.

Heat together the lemon juice and butter and season with salt and pepper to taste. Brush the fish all over with lemon butter and enclose in a wire fish broiler.

Place the fish on the grid. Barbecue for about 8 minutes on each side, turning and brushing with more lemon butter during cooking, until the flesh flakes easily when tested with a fork. Serve with lemon wedges and crusty bread.

68 SPICY GRILLED TROUT

Preparation time:	YOU WILL NEED:
15 minutes	*4 x 225-275 g/8-10 oz trout, cleaned*
	1 tablespoon sweet paprika
Cooking time:	*1½ teaspoons salt*
about 8 minutes	*¼ teaspoon chilli powder*
	4 teaspoons finely chopped onion
Serves 4	*oil for brushing*

Calories:
269 per portion

Wash and dry the trout inside and out with absorbent kitchen paper.

Mix together the paprika, salt and chilli powder. Sprinkle about half this mixture inside the cavities of the 4 trout, then add 1 teaspoon of the chopped onion to each fish. Brush the skin of the fish with oil and sprinkle them with more of the spice mixture.

Barbecue the fish for about 8 minutes, turning them carefully half way through and brushing them with more oil. You could also sprinkle over a little more of the spice mixture, if liked.

The fish are ready when the flesh flakes easily when tested with a fork.

■ COOK'S TIP

If red mullet is not available, substitute the larger grey mullet or red snapper for it in this recipe.

■ COOK'S TIP

For a herb rather than a spice flavour, use finely chopped fresh herbs, such as parsley, thyme, sage and rosemary, instead of the spice mixture. Season the *fish with salt and pepper, then barbecue as above.*

MEAT & POULTRY

Cuts of beef and lamb for barbecue cooking must be good quality and tender. Pork, being a generally tender meat, barbecues well, as does poultry, since most cuts are tender and keep succulent. Follow the recipes in this chapter for some excellent summer recipes involving all these foods - both on and off the barbecue.

69   SPIT-ROASTED LEG OF LAMB

Preparation time:
20 minutes, plus marinating

Cooking time:
1½-2 hours

Serves 4-6

Calories:
716 - 478 per portion

YOU WILL NEED:
2 tablespoons vegetable oil
2 tablespoons white wine
salt and pepper
1 x 1.5-2 kg/3-4 lb leg of lamb
2 garlic cloves, cut into slivers
10 rosemary sprigs
rosemary sprigs, to garnish

Combine the oil, wine and salt and pepper to taste and brush a little over the lamb. Using a small sharp knife, make slits in the lamb skin and insert the garlic slivers and rosemary sprigs.

Put the lamb in a strong polythene bag with the remaining oil and wine mixture. Turn to coat, then leave to marinate in the refrigerator for 2-4 hours, turning from time to time.

Remove the lamb from the bag, reserving the marinade. Insert a rotisserie spit carefully into the lamb (see Cook's Tip below). Scatter a few sprigs of rosemary on the fire for extra flavour and grill the lamb over hot coals for 1 ½-2 hours, basting frequently with the reserved marinade, until the meat is tender but still slightly pink in the centre. Cook for a little longer if well-done lamb is preferred. Serve carved into thick slices, garnished with rosemary sprigs.

70   CARIBBEAN CHICKEN THIGHS

Preparation time:
10 minutes, plus marinating

Cooking time:
15-20 minutes

Serves 6

Calories:
279 per portion

YOU WILL NEED:
6 chicken thighs
1 tablespoon dark rum
1 tablespoon soy sauce
1 small can pineapple rings in natural juice
salt and pepper
4 tablespoons oil

Make two slits on each side of the chicken thighs. Mix the rum, soy sauce and pineapple juice together, brush over the chicken and leave to marinate for 2 hours.

Season lightly with salt and pepper, and grill over hot coals for 15-20 minutes, brushing with oil and turning the chicken frequently. Grill the pineapple rings for 2-3 minutes on each side and serve with the chicken.

■ COOK'S TIP

Make sure that the weight of the leg is evenly distributed. Check that the meat is well balanced by rotating the spit in your hands.

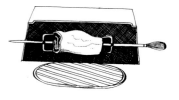

■ COOK'S TIP

Chicken thighs are an economical buy. They can just be brushed with oil and melted butter before grilling, but marinating tenderizes the meat.

71 MINT-STUFFED CHICKEN PORTIONS

Preparation time:
15 minutes

Cooking time:
25 minutes

Serves 4

Calories:
405 per portion

YOU WILL NEED:
4 slices bread
1 lemon
2 teaspoons mint sauce
4 chicken joints
2 tablespoons oil
50 g/2 oz butter, melted

Roughly break the bread and put in a bowl. Coarsely grate the lemon rind and squeeze the juice. Add to the bowl with the mint sauce and mash together with a fork.

Lift the skin from the breast part of the chicken and pack the stuffing under the skin. Grill, bone-side down, over hot coals for about 15 minutes. Brush with oil and melted butter. Turn over and grill for a further 10 minutes. Turn occasionally and brush with butter and oil.

72 BLUE CHEESE CHICKEN

Preparation time:
15 minutes, plus chilling

Cooking time:
30 minutes

Serves 6

Calories:
455 per portion

YOU WILL NEED:
6 chicken breasts
150 ml/¼ pint French dressing
salt and pepper
75 g/3 oz butter
75 g/3 oz blue cheese, finely crumbled
1 tablespoon snipped chives
1 garlic clove, finely chopped
2 tablespoons brandy
FOR THE GARNISH
fresh mint or watercress sprigs
lime or lemon wedges

Place the chicken breasts in a shallow dish, spoon the dressing over them and sprinkle lightly with salt and pepper. Cover and chill for 4 hours, turning the chicken pieces once.

Meanwhile, soften the butter and mix with the cheese, chives, garlic and brandy and season with salt and pepper to taste. Place on a sheet of foil or cling film and form into a roll about 2.5 cm/1 inch in diameter. Chill until firm.

Drain the chicken breasts and grill, skin-side upwards, over hot coals for about 10 minutes. Cut half the cheese butter into twelve pieces. Place one piece on each chicken breast and cook for a further 5 minutes. Turn the breasts, place a piece of butter on each and continue cooking for a further 15 minutes, or until the juices run clear when tested.

Cut the remaining cheese butter into six pieces. Arrange the cooked chicken on a dish and top each with a piece of cheese butter. Garnish with herbs and lime or lemon wedges.

■ COOK'S TIP

You can use bottled mint sauce to flavour the stuffing in this recipe. It tastes even better, however, if you make the sauce yourself with freshly picked mint leaves and white wine vinegar.

■ COOK'S TIP

It is much easier to crumble a piece of blue cheese that has become rather dry than one that is really fresh.

73   EAST INDIAN SATAY

Preparation time:	YOU WILL NEED:
20 minutes, plus marinating	1½ teaspoons ground coriander
	½ teaspoon salt
	1 onion, chopped
Cooking time:	1 garlic clove, chopped
20 minutes	2 tablespoons soy sauce
	1 tablespoon lemon juice
Serves 4	50 g/2 oz roast salted peanuts, ground
Calories:	25 g/1 oz soft brown sugar
428 per portion	3 tablespoons peanut or salad oil
	675 g/1½ lb chicken breasts, boned and cubed
	squares of red, green and yellow pepper
	curly endive leaves

Combine the coriander, salt, onion, garlic, soy sauce, lemon juice, peanuts, sugar and oil in a food processor or blender until smooth. Add pepper to taste. Put the chicken cubes into a shallow dish, pour over the peanut mixture and stir lightly. Cover and leave to marinate for about 4 hours, turning the ingredients occasionally.

Thread the chicken cubes on to four greased skewers, alternating them with squares of pepper. Grill over hot coals for about 20 minutes, until brown but not dry, turning the kebabs frequently and brushing with more of the marinade during cooking.

Line a serving dish with endive leaves and lay the kebabs on top.

■ COOK'S TIP

Mix together 150 ml/¼ pint soured cream and 150 ml/¼ pint plain yogurt. Chop 2 spring onions, 1 garlic clove and 40 g/1½ oz dry roasted peanuts. Stir these into the yogurt mixture, reserving a little to sprinkle on top. Serve with the satay.

74   CRISPY CHICKEN ON STICKS

Preparation time:	YOU WILL NEED:
25 minutes, plus chilling	50 g/2 oz cornflakes, finely crushed
	1 teaspoon curry powder
	½ teaspoon salt
Cooking time:	1 egg, beaten
20 minutes	1 red pepper, seeded
	2 chicken breasts, skinned and boned
Serves 4	50 g/2 oz button mushrooms, halved
Calories:	
142 per portion	

Mix together the cornflake crumbs, curry powder and salt in a bowl. Put the beaten egg in a shallow dish. Slice the pepper flesh thinly, then cut into 2.5 cm/1 inch strips.

Cut the chicken flesh into cubes, about 2.5 cm/1 inch in size. Dip the cubes in the beaten egg and toss them in the cornflake mixture, pressing it on well.

Thread the coated chicken cubes, pepper strips and mushroom halves on about eight wooden sticks or skewers. Place on a baking sheet lined with foil and chill for 2 hours.

Arrange the chicken sticks on a greased barbecue grid. Grill over hot coals for about 20 minutes, turning frequently.

■ COOK'S TIP

Warm pitta bread and a mixed salad including sweetcorn kernels are good with the crispy chicken. Ice-cold lager is a suitable drink to serve with a curry dish. .

75 CRAB-STUFFED TURKEY BREASTS

Preparation time:	YOU WILL NEED:
25 minutes	6 turkey breast fillets
	225 g/8 oz crab sticks, chopped
Cooking time:	75 g/3 oz butter, softened
35 minutes	¼ teaspoon ground nutmeg
	salt and pepper
Serves 6	FOR THE COATING
	25 g/1 oz plain flour
Calories:	1 teaspoon paprika
307 per portion	25 g/1 oz butter, melted

Cut a pocket in each turkey fillet with a sharp knife. Mix together the crab sticks, butter and nutmeg and season with salt and pepper to taste. Use this mixture to fill the turkey fillet cavities.

Combine the flour and paprika. Brush the stuffed fillets with butter, then coat them in the paprika flour.

Enclose in foil parcels and place on the grid. Grill over hot coals for about 30 minutes. Unwrap and place over the coals on the greased grid for a further 5 minutes, turning once, until well browned. Serve immediately.

76 CHICKEN TIKKA

Preparation time:	YOU WILL NEED:
25 minutes, plus	3 chicken breasts, boned
marinating	1 teaspoon salt
	4 tablespoons lemon juice
Cooking time:	1 x 2.5 cm/1 in piece fresh root
10-15 minutes	ginger
	2 garlic cloves
Serves 6	150 ml/¼ pint natural yogurt
	1 teaspoon ground cumin
Calories:	pinch hot curry powder
188 per portion	pinch of cayenne
	orange food colouring (optional)
	100 g/4 oz butter, melted

Remove the skin from the chicken and cut into 2.5 cm/1 inch cubes. Thread loosely on to wooden or metal skewers and sprinkle with salt and lemon juice. Leave for 15-20 minutes.

Peel and grate the ginger and crush the garlic; add to the yogurt with the spices and food colouring, if using. Brush this mixture all over the chicken. Cover and leave to marinate for several hours, overnight if possible.

Grill over hot coals for 10-15 minutes, brushing with melted butter and turning frequently. Serve with wedges of lemon, sliced onion rings and cucumber.

■ COOK'S TIP

Keep a bowl of vegetable oil and a bristle brush near the barbecue for greasing the grid regularly.

■ COOK'S TIP

Another version of tandoori, chicken tikka is traditionally cooked in a clay oven, but cooked over barbecue coals it has just as interesting a flavour.

77 POUSSIN WITH LEMON-BUTTER BASTE

Preparation time:
20 minutes

Cooking time:
10-15 minutes

Serves 6

Calories:
291 per portion

YOU WILL NEED:
3 poussin
75 g/3 oz butter, softened
1 lemon, sliced
6 sprigs fresh tarragon or rosemary
salt and pepper
4 tablespoons sunflower or corn oil

Cut the poussin in half using poultry shears. Open the chicken out and flatten the breast bone. Lift the skin away from the breast and spread softened butter under the skin. Place two lemon slices and two sprigs of fresh herb in each. Sprinkle the birds with salt and pepper and brush with oil.

Grill over hot coals for 10-15 minutes on each side, brushing frequently with oil, until the flesh is firm and the skin crisp.

78 BARBECUED CHICKEN DRUMSTICKS

Preparation time:
10 minutes

Cooking time:
15-20 minutes

Serves 10

Calories:
106 per portion

YOU WILL NEED:
4 tablespoons tomato ketchup
4 tablespoons brown fruity sauce
1 tablespoon malt vinegar
1 tablespoon black treacle
10 chicken drumsticks

Mix the ketchup, fruity sauce, vinegar and treacle together in a small bowl. Brush each drumstick with the glaze.

Grill over hot coals for 15-20 minutes. Turn the chicken frequently and brush with the glaze. Serve with fried onions and hot bread or crisps.

■ COOK'S TIP

Buy young poussin or spring chickens, fresh or frozen, from a butcher or supermarket. Serve half a bird per person.

■ COOK'S TIP

Drumsticks are economical for large barbecue parties; buy them in bulk from a freezer centre and thaw overnight in the refrigerator. If possible, *thaw frozen poultry in a marinade to give it more flavour.*

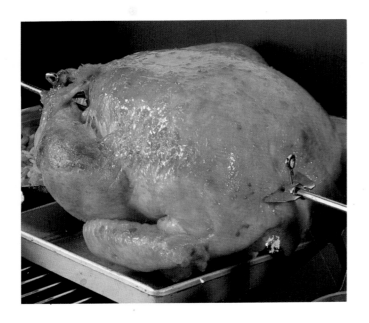

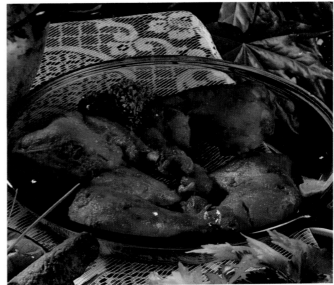

79 SPIT-ROAST TURKEY WITH SPICED APPLE

Preparation time:
15 minutes

Cooking time:
about 3 hours 20 minutes

Serves 8

Calories:
588 per portion

YOU WILL NEED:
1 4.5 kg/10 lb deep basted turkey
2 large cooking apples, peeled
150 ml/¼ pint apple juice
2 tablespoons soft brown sugar
½ teaspoon ground allspice

Ensure that the turkey is completely defrosted, then remove the giblets. Core and chop the apples roughly and use to fill the cavity of the bird. Position the turkey on the spit (see Cook's Tip) and fit the clamps tightly.

Spit-roast the turkey for 20 minutes per 450 g/1 lb, or until a meat thermometer inserted into the thickest part of the thigh registers 90 C/190 F. After the first hour of cooking, brush the skin of the turkey frequently with the apple juice.

When the bird is cooked, scoop the apple filling into a bowl and beat well with the sugar and spice until smooth. Serve the turkey with the spiced apple in a separate bowl.

80 TANDOORI CHICKEN

Preparation time:
15 minutes, plus marinating

Cooking time:
25 minutes

Oven temperature:
200 C/400 F/gas 6
then
180 C/350 F/gas 4

Serves 4

Calories:
784 per portion

YOU WILL NEED:
4 chicken portions, skinned
300 ml/½ pint natural yogurt
2 tablespoons tomato purée
2 teaspoons paprika
1 teaspoon mild chilli powder
1 tablespoon lemon juice
1 teaspoon finely grated lemon rind
1 tablespoon orange juice
1 tablespoon finely grated orange rind
1 teaspoon salt
1 tablespoon grated fresh root ginger
1 teaspoon pepper
2 garlic cloves, finely chopped
few drops red food colouring (optional)

Put the chicken portions in a glass bowl, mix together all the other ingredients and pour over the marinade. Turn the chicken pieces until they are completely coated. Cover and leave to marinate for at least 8 hours.

Lay the chicken pieces in an ovenproof glass dish. Place in a preheated oven for 5 minutes. Reduce the oven temperature and bake for a further 10 minutes. Turn the chicken pieces, and cook for a further 10 minutes. Keep warm or, if required for serving later, leave to cool.

The chicken pieces can be kept in the refrigerator for up to 4 hours before reheating over hot coals for about 10 minutes.

■ COOK'S TIP

Set the turkey, breast side upwards, on a lightly greased grid about 10 cm/4 inches directly above the drip pan. Cover the barbecue and adjust the vents as directed. Roast for 15 minutes per 450 g/1 lb, or until a meat thermometer registers 90 C/190 F, basting frequently with apple juice.

■ COOK'S TIP

Make a yogurt and mint dip to go with this dish. Stir 2 tablespoons chopped mint into 150 ml/¼ pint yogurt. Add a tablespoon of crème fraîche for a richer dip.

81 HONEY BARBECUED CHICKEN

Preparation time: 10 minutes	YOU WILL NEED: 50 g/2 oz butter
	1 onion, finely chopped
Cooking time: 50 minutes	400 g/14 oz canned tomatoes
	2 tablespoons Worcestershire sauce
	1 tablespoon clear honey
Serves 4	salt and pepper
	4 chicken drumsticks, scored
Calories:	TO GARNISH
230 per portion	100 g/4 oz mushrooms
	parsley sprigs
	roast chestnuts (optional)

Put the butter, onion, tomatoes with the canned tomato juices, Worcestershire sauce, honey and salt and pepper to taste in a saucepan. Cook gently for 30 minutes, stirring the sauce occasionally.

Place the drumsticks on the grill pan and spread liberally with the barbecue sauce. Cook the chicken over hot coals or under a preheated moderate grill, for about 10 minutes on each side, basting frequently with more of the sauce. Halfway through the cooking time, put the mushrooms around the chicken. Brush with the sauce and grill until cooked.

Serve the barbecued or grilled chicken on a bed of rice, garnished with the mushrooms and parsley, accompanied by roast chestnuts when in season. Spoon over any remaining sauce.

82 BARBECUED STUFFED CHICKEN BREASTS

Preparation time: 10 minutes	YOU WILL NEED: 40 g/1½ oz butter
	1 onion, finely chopped
Cooking time: 40 minutes	125 g/4 oz brown or white rice, washed and drained
	1 teaspoon turmeric or ½
Serves 4	teaspoon saffron powder
	1 bay leaf
Calories:	3 cloves
271 per portion	2 cardamom pods
	salt
	300 ml/½ pint water
	4 chicken breasts, boned

Melt the butter in a saucepan and fry the onion with the rice until the onion is transparent. Add the turmeric or saffron, bay leaf, cloves, cardamom and salt to taste. Stir in the water and bring to the boil. Simmer gently until the rice is tender and the water has been absorbed.

Put the chicken breasts between sheets of greaseproof paper or clingfilm and beat until thin. Place a little stuffing on each breast and roll up. Secure with a skewer. Grill over hot coals, turning once. Serve with a crisp green salad.

■ COOK'S TIP

If you have a microwave, shelling chestnuts is easy. Just make a slit in each shell, then rinse in cold water and put in a bowl without drying the chestnuts. Cover lightly and cook on high for 5 minutes. When cool enough to handle, remove the shells.

■ COOK'S TIP

If you do not have a metal cutlet bat, you can use a rolling pin or an old-fashioned flat iron to beat the chicken breasts.

83 CHICKEN ON A SPIT

Preparation time:
15 minutes

Cooking time:
1 - 1¼ hours

Serves 4

Calories:
311 per portion

YOU WILL NEED:
1 x 1.5 kg/3 - 3½ lb chicken
juice of ½ lemon
salt and pepper
bunch of mixed fresh herbs
Barbecue sauce (recipe 198)

Wipe the chicken and rub the inside with the lemon juice. Season well inside and out with salt and pepper. Stuff the mixed bunch of fresh herbs into the cavity. Insert the rotisserie spit carefully into the chicken, distributing the weight evenly. Brush with Barbecue sauce and roast over hot coals. Baste with the sauce several times during cooking for a crisp brown chicken. The exact cooking time will depend on the fire and the air temperature.

Serve with barbecued corn on the cob and baked potatoes. Heat any remaining Barbecue sauce to serve with the chicken.

■ COOK'S TIP

When cooking a whole chicken on a spit, truss it securely, keeping the wings and legs close to the body and the neck skin skewered down. Drive the spit in *from a point just in front of the parson's nose and bring it out around the top of the wishbone.*

84 CURRIED-BUTTER CHICKEN DRUMSTICKS

Preparation time:
25 minutes, plus cooling and chilling

Cooking time:
30 minutes

Serves 8

Calories:
309 per portion

YOU WILL NEED:
8 large chicken drumsticks
1 onion, left whole
5 cloves
6 tablespoons dry white wine
12 black peppercorns
2 bay leaves
2 sprigs fresh tarragon
FOR THE CURRIED BUTTER
225 g/8 oz butter, softened
1-2 teaspoons dry mustard
1-3 teaspoons curry powder
1 tablespoon lemon juice
1 tablespoon Worcestershire sauce
salt and pepper

Put the drumsticks in a saucepan with the onion studded with the cloves. Add the white wine, peppercorns, bay leaves and tarragon sprigs, then cover with about 1.2 litres/2 pints cold water. Bring to the boil, then simmer gently for 25 minutes until the drumsticks are cooked through. Leave the drumsticks to cool in the stock.

Mash the butter with the mustard, curry powder, lemon juice and Worcestershire sauce. Season with salt and pepper.

Skin the cooled drumsticks, then spread the butter paste all over them. Wrap a piece of foil around the end of each to make them easier to handle, then arrange the drumsticks on a plate, cover lightly with foil and chill for 3 hours.

Serve the drumsticks straight from the refrigerator.

■ COOK'S TIP

These drumsticks are delicious for a buffet party or a simple summer lunch. Add a touch of ground chilli powder to the butter for a really spicy dish.

85 PARMESAN CHICKEN DRUMSTICKS

Preparation time:
20 minutes, plus
chilling

Cooking time:
30-40 minutes

Serves 4

Calories:
138 per portion

YOU WILL NEED:
25 g/1 oz fresh white breadcrumbs
25 g/1 oz Parmesan cheese, grated
1 tablespoon plain flour
salt and pepper
4 large chicken drumsticks, skinned
1 egg, beaten

Mix together the breadcrumbs and Parmesan cheese. Season the flour with salt and pepper. Coat the chicken drumsticks with the seasoned flour, dip them in the beaten egg, then roll them in the breadcrumb mixture, pressing it on with the fingertips. Make sure the pieces are thoroughly coated, then chill in the refrigerator for 30 minutes.

Grill the drumsticks over hot coals for 30-40 minutes, turning frequently, until tender and cooked through. Serve immediately.

86 SPIT-ROAST DUCKLINGS WITH APRICOT GLAZE

Preparation time:
15 minutes

Cooking time:
1½-2 hours

Serves 8

Calories:
184 per portion

YOU WILL NEED:
2 x 2 kg/4 lb ducklings
salt
225 g/8 oz apricot jam (sieved if
    preferred)
150 ml/¼ pint white vermouth

Defrost the duckling if necessary. Remove the giblets and pat dry inside and out. Sprinkle the birds with salt and truss if necessary. Position on the spit and fit the clamps tightly. Set over a drip pan and spit-roast for 30 minutes.

Combine the apricot jam and vermouth in a pan over a low heat and stir until well blended. Brush the ducks with this mixture and continue cooking for a further 1-1½ hours, basting frequently with the jam, until juices from the thigh run clear when tested with a skewer.

Remove the ducklings from the spit to a serving dish and spoon any remaining baste over the top.

■ COOK'S TIP

Replace the Parmesan cheese in the above recipe with the same quantity of finely chopped peanuts. Be sure to use unsalted peanuts.

■ COOK'S TIP

Always use a drip pan to catch drips from a roast. You can make this by cutting a double thickness of foil 5 cm/2 inches longer than the roast. Fold around a rectangular object to make a dish about 15 cm/6 inches wide and 3 cm/1¼ inches deep.

87 SKEWERED RABBIT WITH REDCURRANT JELLY

Preparation time:
20 minutes

Cooking time:
20 minutes

Serves 4

Calories:
214 per portion

YOU WILL NEED:
450 g/1 lb boneless rabbit meat
salt and pepper
3 tablespoons redcurrant jelly
4 teaspoons olive oil

Trim and cut the rabbit meat into serving-sized pieces. Thread on to skewers and season with salt and pepper. Melt the redcurrant jelly in a pan over a low heat. Brush the meat lightly with the redcurrant jelly and then with the oil.

Grill over medium to hot coals for 15 minutes, turning from time to time. Serve with additional redcurrant jelly and jacket potatoes.

88 RABBIT WITH MUSTARD

Preparation time:
10 minutes

Cooking time:
about 30 minutes

Serves 4

Calories:
596 per portion

YOU WILL NEED:
1 rabbit, cut into 6 joints
salt and pepper
50 g/2 oz butter
2 tablespoons oil
1 bay leaf
1 tablespoon chopped fresh thyme
2 tablespoons coarse-grain mustard

Sprinkle the rabbit joints with salt and pepper and place the remaining ingredients in a small pan.

Grill the rabbit over medium-hot coals and place the pan of sauce on the grid. Turn the rabbit and brush with the sauce frequently. Continue to cook for about 30 minutes or until the flesh feels firm and the juices run clear when the meat is pierced with a skewer.

Serve the rabbit with grilled apple rings, accompanied by any remaining sauce.

■ COOK'S TIP

In some country markets you may be able to buy wild rabbit which has a more pronounced gamey taste and darker meat than the farmed rabbit.

■ COOK'S TIP

Ask your butcher to joint the rabbit for you, or use poultry shears. The meat can be dry so baste it frequently with this not-too-hot mustard glaze.

89   CHINESE ORANGE DUCK

Preparation time:
15 minutes, plus
marinating

Cooking time:
about 1 hour

Serves 4

Calories:
489 per portion

YOU WILL NEED:
4 spring onions
pinch of ground ginger
1 teaspoon turmeric
2 tablespoons dark soy sauce
4 tablespoons fine-cut marmalade
salt and pepper
1 x 2-2.5 kg/4-5 lb duck, quartered
1 orange

Trim and finely chop the spring onions, putting them in a large shallow dish with the ginger, turmeric, soy sauce and marmalade; mix together well. Season the duck with salt and pepper, add to the dish and brush the sauce all over the duck until well coated. Cover and leave to marinate for 4 hours.

Place the grill about 10 cm/4 inches above medium-hot coals and cook the duck, bone side down, for 15 minutes. Turn the duck over and brush with the sauce. Cook for a further 10-15 minutes, taking care not to burn the skin. Turn over again and cook for a further 15-20 minutes or until the flesh feels firm. Turn the duck over and crisp the skin for the last 5-10 minutes.

Slice the orange, brush with marinade and grill for 5 minutes. Use to garnish the serving dish of duck quarters. Serve with Chinese leaves.

90   SKEWERED LAMB MEATBALLS

Preparation time:
30 minutes, plus
soaking

Cooking time:
15-20 minutes

Serves 6

Calories:
392 per portion

YOU WILL NEED:
100 g/4 oz sultanas
675 g/1½ lb boned shoulder of
    lamb
225 g/8 oz fresh white
    breadcrumbs
2 eggs, beaten
salt and pepper
1 tablespoon curry powder
2 onions, sliced into rings

Soak the sultanas in water for 1 hour; drain.

Mince the lamb and mix with the breadcrumbs, sultanas, beaten eggs, seasoning and curry powder. Mix together thoroughly, then shape into twelve meatballs. Arrange the meatballs on six skewers, alternating with the onion rings.

Grill the skewered meatballs over hot coals for 15-20 minutes, turning frequently. Serve on a bed of savoury rice.

■ COOK'S TIP

Use poultry shears or ask the butcher to cut the duck into quarters. The duck should be well cooked until the skin is crisp - delicious with the sticky sweet sauce.

■ COOK'S TIP

Traditionally these meatballs are enclosed in animal membrane known as a caul before grilling, which your butcher may be able to supply, but it is optional, as the meatballs should hold together without it.

91 LAMB STEAKS WITH FRUIT SIDE DISH

Preparation time:
30 minutes, plus
marinating

Cooking time:
35 minutes

Serves 4

Calories:
460 per portion

YOU WILL NEED:
4 leg bone lamb steaks
425g/15 oz can red kiwi fruit slices
2 teaspoons curry powder
1 onion, finely chopped
2 tablespoons vinegar
1 tablespoon oil
pinch of ground cinnamon
1 orange
1 red-skinned dessert apple
225 g/8 oz white cabbage, shredded
2 tablespoons flaked almonds, toasted
1 tablespoon French dressing

Put the steaks in a shallow dish. Drain the syrup from the kiwi fruit, take 4 tablespoons of the syrup and mix with the curry powder, onion, vinegar, oil and cinnamon. Pour over the steaks, cover and leave to marinate for at least 4 hours.

For the side dish, peel the orange and divide into slices, discarding any pith. Cut each slice in half. Core and slice the apple. Mix the cabbage, apple, orange, kiwi fruit slices and almonds in a bowl. Stir together 1 tablespoon of the remaining kiwi fruit syrup and the dressing and pour over the ingredients.

Drain the lamb steaks. Enclose each one in a foil parcel. Arrange the foil parcels on the barbecue grid. Grill over hot coals for about 30 minutes. Unwrap, arrange on the greased grid and grill for 5 more minutes, turning once.

Serve with the remaining marinade and the side dish.

92 LAMB AND PEPPER KEBABS

Preparation time:
20 minutes, plus
marinating

Cooking time:
about 20 minutes

Serves 4

Calories:
362 per portion

YOU WILL NEED:
450 g/1 lb boneless lean lamb
1 tablespoon oil
1 tablespoon wine vinegar
¼ teaspoon dried basil
salt and pepper
1 small green pepper, seeded
1 small red pepper, seeded
2 small onions, quartered

Cut the lamb into sixteen cubes and place in a shallow dish. Mix together the oil, vinegar, basil and a little salt and pepper. Pour over the lamb, cover and leave to marinate for at least 8 hours.

Cut the pepper flesh into squares. Drain the lamb cubes and thread them on to four oiled skewers, alternating with the pepper and onion quarters. Place the kebabs on a greased grid. Grill over hot coals for about 20 minutes, turning frequently and brushing with more of the marinade from time to time.

COOK'S TIP

Apricots are another fruit that is particularly good with kebabs. Dried apricots have a much better flavour and texture than canned ones.

COOK'S TIP

Long-handled tongs are an invaluable barbecue accessory for turning kebabs and other items safely. When buying a pair, check there are no rough edges which could catch on or tear the food.

93 WANAKA BARBECUED LAMB

Preparation time:
15 minutes, plus
marinating

Cooking time:
about 40 minutes

Serves 6

Calories:
381 per portion

YOU WILL NEED:
2 breasts of lamb
225 g/8 oz plum jam
4 tablespoons tomato ketchup
1 tablespoon Worcestershire sauce
1 tablespoon mild mustard

Using a pair of scissors or a sharp knife, cut the breasts of lamb between the bones. Put the ribs in a large pan and cover with cold water. Boil steadily for 20 minutes then drain.

Meanwhile, mix together the jam, ketchup, Worcestershire sauce and mustard in a large bowl. Add the ribs while they are still hot and stir well to coat thoroughly. Cover and leave to marinate for 2 hours if time permits, although the ribs can be cooked at once if necessary.

Thread the ribs of lamb on to pairs of long greased skewers held 5 cm/2 inches apart so that they are easy to turn during cooking. Place on a greased grid and grill over hot coals for about 20 minutes, turning frequently and brushing with any remaining marinade.

94 SPIT-ROAST BONED LAMB WITH BEANS

Preparation time:
15 minutes, plus
soaking

Cooking time:
about 3 hours

Serves 8

Calories:
914 per portion

YOU WILL NEED:
225 g/8 oz dried haricot beans
salt and pepper
2 bay leaves
2 tablespoons oil
1 large onion, sliced
1 garlic clove, finely chopped
2 tablespoons chopped fresh herbs
1 x 2 kg/4 lb leg or shoulder of
    lamb, boned, rolled and tied
175 g/6 oz redcurrant jelly
4 tablespoons bottled barbecue
    sauce

Soak the beans in cold water overnight. Drain, place in a pan with fresh water to cover and bring to the boil. Boil rapidly for 10 minutes, then skim. Season with salt and pepper and add the bay leaves. Bring to the boil, cover and simmer 30 minutes.

Heat the oil and fry the onion and garlic lightly. Stir in to the beans, cover and cook for 20 minutes, or until the beans are tender. Drain off any excess liquid, adjust the seasoning and stir in the herbs. Transfer to another pan and keep warm.

Season the meat and place on the spit over a drip pan (see recipe 86). Barbecue for 25-30 minutes per 450 g/1 lb, or until a meat thermometer inserted deep into the meat registers 90 C/190 F. Melt the redcurrant jelly and barbecue sauce together and baste the lamb with the mixture during the last 30 minutes of cooking time. Serve the lamb with the beans.

■ COOK'S TIP

Breast of lamb is an economical cut and can be treated like pork spareribs, although it is more usually boned, stuffed and rolled before roasting or braising.

■ COOK'S TIP

When spit-roasting, always have a small drip tray to catch the juice from the meat and ensure that the joint is correctly balanced to avoid strain on the motor turning it round. Jerky, uneven movements will not produce evenly browned food and will eventually break the rotisserie.

95 KIBBEH

Preparation time:
20 minutes, plus
soaking

Cooking time:
about 10 minutes

Serves 8

Calories:
118 per portion

YOU WILL NEED:
175 g/6 oz finely ground couscous
1 small onion, grated
225 g/8 oz minced lamb
1½ teaspoons salt
½ teaspoon ground black pepper
½ teaspoon ground cinnamon
½ teaspoon paprika

Place the couscous in a large bowl, cover with cold water and leave to soak for 30 minutes. Drain, pressing out as much moisture as possible.

Place the onion in a bowl with the lamb and spices. Knead together, then knead in the couscous. Knead for about 10 minutes until the mixture forms a soft dough, to ensure that it will not be coarse when cooked. Using damp hands, divide the mixture into eight portions and roll between the palms of your hands to give long, oval, cigar-shaped sausages. Place a metal skewer on each one and wrap the mixture tightly around it.

Grill over hot coals, turning frequently, for about 10 minutes. Serve with a crisp salad.

96 TURKISH SHISH KEBAB

Preparation time:
20 minutes, plus
marinating

Cooking time:
about 10 minutes

Makes 8 kebabs

Calories:
309 per portion

YOU WILL NEED:
2 onions
125 ml/¼ pint olive oil
rind and juice of 1 lemon
1 teaspoon ground cinnamon
½ teaspoon salt
pepper
1 kg/2 lb lean shoulder of lamb, cubed
4 courgettes

Peel the onions and blend them in a liquidizer or food processor or grate finely. Press the onion purée through a sieve to extract the juice.

In a large bowl, mix the onion juice with the oil, lemon juice and rind, cinnamon, salt and a good shake of pepper. Add the meat and turn until well coated. Cover and leave to marinate for 3-4 hours or overnight if possible.

Cut away six long, thin strips of courgette peel and slice the courgettes so that they look like wheels. Thread the meat and courgettes together on eight metal or wooden skewers and grill over hot coals, turning frequently, for about 10 minutes.

Serve with saffron rice and salad.

■ COOK'S TIP

Kibbeh are Lebanese minced lamb kebabs. Buy finely minced lamb and if possible mince it again (or blend in a food processor). The finer it is minced, the better the mixture will hold together. Couscous is a type of semolina available in most supermarkets and health food shops.

■ COOK'S TIP

A canelle knife is the ideal tool to use for cutting away strips of courgette peel neatly. It is equally effective with cucumber and citrus fruit.

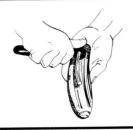

97 LAMB CHOPS WITH GREEN PEPPERCORN GLAZE

Preparation time:
20 minutes

Cooking time:
20 minutes

Serves 4

Calories:
237 per portion

YOU WILL NEED:
4 lean lamb chops
4 teaspoons dried green
    peppercorns, crushed
½ teaspoon salt
1 tablespoon oil
4 tablespoons redcurrant jelly

Trim any excess fat from the lamb chops. Crush the peppercorns and mix them with the salt. Press well on to both sides of the lamb.

Brush the lamb with oil and grill over hot coals for 10 minutes on each side.

Put the redcurrant jelly in a small saucepan and heat gently. Pour over both sides of the lamb just before serving.

98 ROSEMARY AND GARLIC-STUDDED SHOULDER

Preparation time:
15 minutes

Cooking time:
about 40 minutes,
plus resting

Serves 6-8

Calories:
437 per portion

YOU WILL NEED:
1 small shoulder of lamb
6 fresh rosemary sprigs
6 fresh thyme sprigs
4 tablespoons olive oil
3 garlic cloves, sliced
salt and pepper

Trim any excess fat from the lamb and cut two or three deep slashes right through the meat to the bone. Place a sprig each of rosemary and thyme in each cut. Make small slits in the meat using just the point of a knife and place a thin slice of garlic in each. Brush with oil and sprinkle with salt and pepper.

You will need a deep charcoal fire initially but if the coals begin to get too hot, spread them out thinly. Place the grid about 12 cm/5 inches away from the coals, moving it nearer or further depending on the heat. Grill the meat over medium hot coals, turning every 10 minutes and brushing with oil.

Test the joint after 40 minutes by pressing the thickest part of the meat. It should feel quite firm when cooked and the juices should run clear or slightly pink, but not bloody, when the meat is pierced with a skewer. Leave the shoulder to rest for 10-15 minutes before carving.

■ COOK'S TIP

Dried green peppercorns are milder and sweeter than black ones - delicious sprinkled on any meat. You will find them in most delicatessens.

■ COOK'S TIP

A shoulder of lamb is the only large joint that is suitable for grilling over the coals without a spit roaster. The meat will cook crisply on the outside but be juicy pink inside. Great care must be taken not to burn the outside before the joint is cooked through.

99   BARBECUED GIGOT CHOPS

Preparation time:	YOU WILL NEED:
5 minutes	*4 gigot lamb chops*
	oil
Cooking time:	*pepper and salt*
about 25 minutes	*chopped fresh parsley*
Serves 4	
Calories:	
424 per portion	

Trim any excess fat from the chops. Brush them with oil and season with pepper.

Place the chops on the barbecue grid and grill over hot coals for about 25 minutes, turing occasionally.

Sprinkle the chops with a little salt and arrange them on a warmed serving plate garnished wish parsley. Sprinkle a little chopped parsley on top of each chop and serve with Barbecue sauce (recipe 198).

100   SPICY BARBECUED LAMB

Preparation time:	YOU WILL NEED:
15 minutes, plus	*1 x 2 kg/4 lb breast of lamb*
cooling and	*lemon wedges, to garnish*
marinating	*FOR THE CIDER MARINADE*
	150 ml/¼ pint dry cider
Cooking time:	*2 tablespoons Worcestershire sauce*
45-60 minutes	*1 tablespoon brown sugar*
	2 tablespoons oil
Serves 4	*2 tablespoons wine or cider vinegar*
	1 onion, finely chopped
Calories:	*½ teaspoon dried rosemary*
1257 per portion	*salt and pepper*

Remove any excess fat from the lamb and cut the meat in strips between the bones with a sharp knife.

Place all the marinade ingredients in a pan and bring to the boil. Simmer gently for 3-4 minutes then leave to cool. Put the lamb in a bowl, pour the marinade over and leave to marinate in the refrigerator for at least three hours, turning occasionally.

Place the lamb on the barbecue grid and grill over hot coals until crisp, 45-60 minutes, basting occasionally with the marinade.

Serve hot, piled on a large platter and garnished with lemon wedges. Heat the remaining marinade and serve separately.

■ COOK'S TIP

A leg of lamb is called a gigot in Scotland. In other places butchers may use the term leg chops to describe this prime cut.

■ COOK'S TIP

If you prefer not to use any alcohol, replace the cider in the marinade with the same quantity of unsweetened apple juice.

101 BARBECUED LAMB CUTLETS IN RED WINE

Preparation time: 5 minutes, plus marinating	YOU WILL NEED: *8 lamb cutlets, about 2.5 cm/ 1 inch thick* *175 ml/6 fl oz red wine*
Cooking time: 15-20 minutes	*2 tablespoons olive oil* *6 tablespoons finely chopped fresh mint*
Serves 4	*salt and pepper* FOR THE GARNISH
Calories: 416 per portion	*parsley sprigs* *tomato wedges*

Place the cutlets in a shallow dish; mix together the wine, oil and chopped mint and pour over the meat. Cover and leave in a cool place for 1 hour, turning after 30 minutes.

Remove the lamb from the marinade and grill over hot coals for 7-10 minutes each side, according to whether you like lamb rare or well done. Baste with any leftover marinade before turning.

Sprinkle with salt and pepper and serve very hot, garnished with the parsley and tomato wedges. If liked, make a small bowl of Yogurt marinade (recipe 194) to serve as an accompanying dip.

102 LAMB KEBABS MARINATED IN YOGURT

Preparation time: 15 minutes, plus marinating	YOU WILL NEED: *1 kg/2 lb boned leg of lamb, cut into 2 cm/¾ inch cubes* *1 quantity Yogurt marinade (recipe 194)*
Cooking time: 10-20 minutes	*1 bunch fresh coriander leaves, coarsely chopped*
Serves 4	*lime wedges to serve*
Calories: 432 per portion	

Thread the lamb cubes on to long skewers and place them in a shallow dish or roasting tin. Pour over the marinade, turn the skewers two or three times, then cover and leave in a cool place for at least 12 hours or, ideally, chill in the refrigerator for 24 hours.

Remove the skewers from the marinade, gently shaking off any excess liquids then grill the kebabs over hot coals for 10 minutes for rare meat or 20 minutes for well done. Turn once half way through the cooking time and baste with the remaining marinade.

Cover a serving dish with a layer of the chopped coriander leaves, then push the meat off the skewers on to the coriander. Serve with the lime wedges.

■ COOK'S TIP

It's worth growing a selection of mints. For this dish try a mix of two or three different mints, such as apple, lemon, orange or peppermint.

■ COOK'S TIP

Some butchers sell the boned neck of lamb as lamb fillet. This is ideal for the dish and much more economical.

103 LAMB KEBABS WITH MINT

Preparation time:
15 minutes, plus
marinating

Cooking time:
10-15 minutes

Serves 4

Calories:
399 per portion

YOU WILL NEED:
750 g/1½ lb boned leg of lamb,
 trimmed and cut into 2.5 cm/
 1 inch cubes
½ onion, finely sliced
1 garlic clove, crushed
2 tablespoons chopped fresh mint
1 teaspoon chopped fresh parsley
4 tablespoons olive oil
4 tablespoons red wine
2 corn cobs (see Cook's Tip below)
mint sprigs, to garnish

Place the lamb, onion and garlic in a large shallow bowl. Add the herbs, oil and wine and stir well to mix. Cover and leave to marinate in the refrigerator for 4-6 hours or overnight, turning the meat once or twice.

Slice the corn cobs crossways into 2.5-cm/1-inch pieces.

Lift the lamb from the marinade and thread the cubes loosely on to oiled kebab skewers alternately with the corn; reserve the marinade.

Grill the kebabs over hot coals, turning frequently and brushing with the reserved marinade, for 10-15 minutes or until tender. Serve garnished with mint sprigs.

104 GREEK KEBABS

Preparation time:
20 minutes, plus
marinating

Cooking time:
10-15 minutes

Serves 4

Calories:
784 per portion

YOU WILL NEED:
4 tablespoons vegetable oil
2 tablespoons white wine vinegar
2 tablespoons lemon juice
1 garlic clove, crushed
1 small onion, finely chopped
salt and pepper
1.25 kg/2½ lb fillet end of leg of
 lamb, boned, trimmed and cut
 into 2.5 cm/1 inch cubes
2 onions, divided into leaves and
 cut into 2.5 cm/1 inch squares
8 bay leaves
FOR THE GARNISH
lemon wedges
bay leaves
parsley sprigs

Place the oil in a large shallow bowl with the vinegar, lemon juice, garlic, chopped onion and salt and pepper. Add the lamb, stir to coat, cover and leave to marinate in the refrigerator for at least 2 hours, turning several times so the cubes remain coated in the marinade.

Blanch the onion pieces for 1 minute in boiling water then drain. Lift the lamb cubes from the marinade, reserving the marinade. Thread the meat alternately with the bay leaves and onion pieces on to four oiled kebab skewers.

Cook the kebabs over hot coals, turning and basting with the reserved marinade, for 10-15 minutes or until tender. Serve garnished with lemon wedges, bay leaves and parsley.

COOK'S TIP

To prepare the corn cobs, remove the leafy husks and pull off the silky threads. Brittle husks denote the cobs are not freshly picked.

COOK'S TIP

Have a Greek-style barbecue with a feta cheese salad, hot pitta bread, green olives and small bowls of hummus and taramasalata. Serve a retsina wine.

105 RELISHBURGERS

Preparation time:
20 minutes, plus
chilling

Cooking time:
about 15 minutes

Serves 12

Calories:
185 per portion

YOU WILL NEED:
100 g/4 oz fresh white breadcrumbs
1 kg/2 lb minced beef
3 tablespoons bottled barbecue
  relish
1 onion, finely chopped
1 egg
rolled oats for coating
parsley sprigs to garnish

Place the breadcrumbs in a bowl and add the meat, relish, onion and egg; mix thoroughly. Divide into twelve equal portions and shape each into a burger about 2.5 cm/1 inch thick. Coat with the oats, patting them on firmly.

Line a baking sheet with foil, put the relishburgers on top, cover with more foil and crimp all round to make an airtight parcel. Chill thoroughly.

Unwrap and arrange the chilled burgers on an oiled grid. Grill over hot coals for about 15 minutes, turning carefully half-way through cooking. Garnish with parsley and serve in buns accompanied by a cucumber salad and extra relish.

106 STEAKS WITH APRICOT TOPPERS

Preparation time:
10 minutes

Cooking time:
about 8 minutes

Serves 4

Calories:
297 per portion

YOU WILL NEED:
40 g/1½ oz savoury butter with
  herbs and garlic
4 sirloin steaks, about 100 g/4 oz
  each
8 canned apricot halves and 2
  tablespoons apricot syrup from
  the can

Cut the block of savoury butter into eight pieces. Brush the steaks with the apricot syrup and arrange in a foil grill tray. Cook over hot coals for about 4 minutes then turn the steaks.

If necessary, cut a sliver from the rounded side of each apricot half so that it will stand firmly with the hollow upwards. Position two apricot 'cups' on each steak and put a piece of savoury butter in each hollow.

Cook for a further 4 minutes, or until the steak is done to your taste and the savoury butter in the apricot cup begins to melt.

■ COOK'S TIP

Prepare a batch of burgers in advance, wrap in foil and freeze. Thaw thoroughly before cooking on a barbecue.

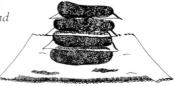

■ COOK'S TIP

Packets of prepared savoury butter are sold in large supermarkets but it is easy to make up different blends, using the appropriate fresh herbs.

107 RED WINE MARINATED BEEF

Preparation time:
15 minutes, plus
marinating

Cooking time:
14-18 minutes

Serves 4

Calories:
270 per portion

YOU WILL NEED:
FOR THE RED WINE MARINADE
1 onion
1 carrot
½ teaspoon dried parsley
½ teaspoon dried thyme
1 bay leaf
6 peppercorns
2 tablespoons oil
150 ml/¼ pint red wine

4 thick slices beef skirt or flank
  steak
salt and pepper
oil

Slice the onion and carrot. Place in a large shallow dish with the herbs, spices, oil and wine. Add the beef and turn it in the marinade until well coated. Leave to marinate for at least 6 hours, overnight if possible.

Drain the meat, season with salt and pepper and sear over hot coals for 2-3 minutes on each side. Brush with oil; move to less intense heat (or move the grill-rack higher up) and cook for 5-6 minutes on each side. Serve with onion rings.

108 QUICK-FRIED STEAKS WITH BARBECUE GLAZE

Preparation time:
10 minutes

Cooking time:
10-12 minutes

Serves 6

Calories:
181 per portion

YOU WILL NEED:
FOR THE BARBECUE GLAZE
1 tablespoon malt vinegar
1 teaspoon mild English mustard
1 tablespoon dark brown sugar
pinch paprika
2 teaspoons Worcestershire sauce
1 teaspoon soy sauce
3 tablespoons tomato ketchup

6 quick-fry tenderized steaks
salt and pepper
oil

Mix the barbecue glaze ingredients together, adding a little water to make a thin sauce. Sprinkle the steaks with salt and pepper and brush with oil.

Sear the steaks over medium-hot coals for 1 minute on each side; brush with the glaze and cook for a further 4-5 minutes on each side, brushing frequently with the glaze.

Serve with a crisp salad and the remaining glaze.

■ COOK'S TIP

*Beef skirt or flank is ideal
for barbecuing, but it is best
eaten rare or medium rare
as it is lean and can become
dry. This marinade helps to
tenderize the meat.*

■ COOK'S TIP

*Choose thick, tenderized
quick-fry steaks, or they
will dry out and char before
they are properly cooked.*

109 MALAY BEEF

Preparation time:	YOU WILL NEED:
10 minutes, plus	*300 ml/½ pint milk*
marinating	*50 g/2 oz desiccated coconut*
	1 x 2.5 cm/1 inch piece fresh root
Cooking time:	*ginger*
6-8 minutes	*2 small chilli peppers*
	1 tablespoon dark brown sugar
Serves 4	*½ teaspoon cayenne*
	4 small quick-fry tenderized beef
Calories:	*steaks*
294 per portion	*salt and pepper*

Place the milk and coconut in a small pan; heat gently. Peel and chop the ginger very finely. Chop the chilli peppers. Add the ginger, chilli, sugar and cayenne to the milk then remove from the heat. Reserve 4 tablespoons of the marinade.

Cut the steak into long 2.5 cm/1 inch wide strips. Season lightly with salt and pepper and lay the meat in the milk. Leave to marinate for at least 2 hours, overnight if possible.

Thread the meat on to wooden or metal skewers or place carefully over a fine grid. Grill over hot coals, basting with the marinade occasionally, for 3-4 minutes on each side. Heat the remaining marinade and serve with the meat.

110 STEAK AU POIVRE

Preparation time:	YOU WILL NEED:
20 minutes	*4 tablespoons black peppercorns*
	salt
Cooking time:	*4 rump steaks*
about 10 minutes,	*oil*
or to taste	*single cream (optional)*
Serves 4	
Calories:	
252 per portion	

Crush the peppercorns roughly. Hammer them with a rolling pin through several sheets of greaseproof paper or process briefly in the dry foods attachment of a liquidizer.

Place the peppercorns on a large plate and press the steaks hard down on to them, lightly coating both sides. Sprinkle the meat with the salt and brush with a little oil. Sear the steaks over very hot coals until brown, turning them with tongs so as not to dislodge too many peppercorns.

Cook to taste. Drizzle with a little single cream as you serve them, if liked.

■ COOK'S TIP

This dish needs a little preparation - preferably the day before - and then it cooks quickly over the hot coals. Coconut and peppers give this a creamy, hot flavour. Don't worry if the marinade curdles; it still tastes good.

■ COOK'S TIP

If you are using a liquidizer to crush the peppercorns, take care that you do not crush them to a powder.

111 HAMBURGERS WITH PIZZAIOLA SAUCE

Preparation time:
15 minutes

Cooking time:
about 30 minutes

Serves 4

Calories:
348 per portion

YOU WILL NEED:
450 g/1 lb minced beef
1 onion, finely grated
1 egg, lightly beaten
salt and pepper
2 teaspoons Worcestershire sauce
FOR THE SAUCE
2 teaspoons oil
2 medium onions, minced
2 garlic cloves, minced
2 small green peppers, cored,
    seeded and sliced into rings
50 g/2 oz mushrooms, chopped
1 x 400 g/14 oz can red tomatoes
2 teaspoons dried marjoram
dash hot chilli sauce

Place the beef in a bowl with the onion and mix in the egg, salt and pepper to taste and Worcestershire sauce. Divide into four and shape into hamburgers about 2 cm/¾ inch thick.

Heat the oil in a frying pan. Add the onions and garlic and fry until golden. Add the pepper rings and continue cooking for 15 minutes. Stir in the mushrooms, tomatoes with their juice and the marjoram. Season to taste with the chilli sauce, salt and pepper. Cover and continue cooking for 10 minutes.

Meanwhile, grill or barbecue the hamburgers for about 15 minutes, or to taste. Arrange on a hot serving dish and pour the sauce over them. Serve with a crisp green salad.

▨ COOK'S TIP

This popular Italian sauce may also be served with grilled steaks as well as different types of pasta.

112 DEVILLED STEAKS

Preparation time:
5 minutes

Cooking time:
about 10 minutes

Serves 4

Calories:
281 per portion

YOU WILL NEED:
4 rump steaks, trimmed
pepper
4 teaspoons French mustard
4 tablespoons soft light brown sugar
salt
parsley sprigs, to garnish (optional)

Season the steaks with pepper. Combine the mustard and sugar and spread half the mixture over one side of each steak.

Grill the steaks over hot coals for 5 minutes. Turn over and spread with the remaining mustard mixture. Cook for a further 5 minutes or until the steaks are cooked according to taste. Season with salt to taste. Serve the steaks garnished with parsley sprigs, if using.

▨ COOK'S TIP

Serve Devilled steaks with a mushroom and tomato salad sprinkled with chopped basil and with Cream cheese-stuffed potatoes (recipe 146).

113 BEEF TERIYAKI

Preparation time:
15 minutes, plus
marinating

Cooking time:
6-8 minutes, or to
taste

Serves 4

Calories:
281 per portion

YOU WILL NEED:
*4 tablespoons soy sauce (see
   Cook's Tip below)*
2 tablespoons dry sherry
*2 teaspoons chopped fresh root
   ginger*
1 garlic clove, crushed
4 rump or sirloin steaks
FOR THE DIPPING SAUCE
125 ml/4 fl oz soy sauce
4 tablespoons dry sherry
3 spring onions, finely chopped
*2 teaspoons chopped fresh root
   ginger*
1 teaspoon lemon juice

Mix the soy sauce, sherry, ginger and garlic together in a
shallow dish. Add the steaks and marinate at room temperature
for 2 hours, turning occasionally.

Remove the steaks from the marinade, using a slotted
spoon. Reserve the marinade. Grill the meat over hot coals,
about 15 cm/6 inches above the fire. Turning and basting with
the reserved marinade, cook for 3-4 minutes on each side for
medium steaks or longer if you prefer well done.

While the steaks are cooking, combine all the sauce
ingredients and spoon into individual small bowls. Slice the
cooked steaks into strips and serve with the dipping sauce.

114 CARPETBAG STEAK

Preparation time:
20 minutes

Cooking time:
19-24 minutes, or to
taste

Serves 4

Calories:
558 per portion

YOU WILL NEED:
1 kg/2 lb piece rump steak
*225 g/8 oz canned oysters in brine,
   drained*
2 tablespoons lemon juice
salt and pepper
3 tablespoons vegetable oil
FOR THE GARNISH
chopped fresh parsley (optional)
lemon wedges

Slit the steak horizontally, leaving one long edge uncut so it
can be opened out like a book. Place the oysters on one cut
surface of the meat and sprinkle with the lemon juice. Cover
with the other half of the steak, then sew up the three cut
sides, using a trussing needle and fine string.

Season the steak with salt and pepper and brush with the
oil. Sear the meat over very hot coals for 2 minutes on each
side, then adjust the height of the grill and cook for a further
15-20 minutes over a low heat or until the steak is cooked
according to taste. Season the steak with salt.

Remove the string and cut the steak crossways into four
slices. Serve garnished with lemon wedges and chopped parsley
if using.

■ COOK'S TIP

*Japanese soy sauce should
be used in this recipe if
possible. It is available from
Oriental grocers and
specialist food shops.*

■ COOK'S TIP

*For those who are allergic
to oysters, replace with a
similar-sized can of mussels
or use chilled shelled
mussels now available in
most supermarkets.*

115 SPIT-ROASTED BEEF

Preparation time:
15 minutes, plus
marinating

Cooking time:
about 1½ hours

Serves 6-8

Calories:
671 - 503 per
portion

YOU WILL NEED:
1.5-2 kg/3-4 lb sirloin of beef,
   rolled and tied
3 tablespoons olive oil
1 tablespoon lemon juice
3 large onions, sliced
melted butter for basting
1 tablespoon plain flour
salt and pepper

Rub the beef with the olive oil and sprinkle with the lemon juice. Place half the onion slices in a dish, put the beef on top and cover with the remaining onion slices. Leave to marinate for at least 3 hours. Discard the onions or reserve and serve, fried, with the roast beef.

Insert the spit into the beef (see recipes 69 and 94)) and roast over hot coals. Place a drip pan beneath the spit to catch the meat juices and baste frequently with melted butter. After about 20 minutes, when the beef is well browned, dust it with the flour. Allow the flour to dry to a crust then baste again. Roast the beef for a further 1¼ hours, basting from time to time, until the meat is tender and cooked according to taste. Season with salt and pepper.

To serve, remove the string and carve the beef into thin slices. Skim the fat from the juices in the drip pan and pour the juices over the beef.

116 ITALIAN-STYLE CHEESEBURGERS

Preparation time:
15 minutes, plus
chilling

Cooking time:
about 13 minutes

Serves 4

Calories:
327 per portion

YOU WILL NEED:
450 g/1 lb lean minced beef
1 onion, finely grated
1 garlic clove, crushed
1 tablespoon tomato purée
½ teaspoon dried oregano
salt and pepper
vegetable oil
75 g/3 oz mozzarella cheese, cut
   into 4 equal slices
4 tomato slices

Put the beef, onion, garlic, tomato purée, oregano and salt and pepper in a large bowl and stir well to mix. Using floured hands, divide the mixture into four equal portions and shape into patties. Cover and chill in the refrigerator for up to 12 hours until ready to cook.

Brush the burgers all over with oil and cook over hot coals for 5 minutes. Turn and, after a few minutes, place a slice of cheese on top of each. Cook for a further 8 minutes or until the cheese is melted and the hamburger is cooked according to taste. Top each burger with a tomato slice before serving.

■ COOK'S TIP

Try adding 1 teaspoon of dry mustard to the flour before dusting the beef. Serve the beef with horseradish sauce and jacket potatoes.

■ COOK'S TIP

Serve the cheeseburgers in hamburger buns with tomato relish and a green salad. Slices of Cheddar cheese may be used instead of the mozzarella.

117 GUINNESS MARINATED STEAKS

Preparation time:
15 minutes, plus
marinating

Cooking time:
6-12 minutes

Serves 4

Calories:
495 per portion

YOU WILL NEED:
4 sirloin steaks, about 225 g/8 oz
  each
1 quantity Guinness marinade
  (recipe 195)
1 tablespoon olive oil
pepper
coarsely ground sea salt

Trim all but a thin margin of fat off the steaks, then place
them in a shallow dish. Pour the marinade over, cover and
leave to marinate in a cool place for at least 6 hours, turning
the steaks at half-time.

Five minutes before cooking the steaks, remove from the
marinade and pat dry with absorbent kitchen paper. Strain the
marinade into a small heavy-based saucepan and boil rapidly
until reduced by nearly half. This can be done either in the
kitchen or on the barbecue.

Brush one side of each steak with a little olive oil and a
little of the reduced marinade, then grill, oiled-side down, over
hot coals for 3-4 minutes for rare steaks, 4-5 minutes for
medium, or 5-6 minutes for well done. Baste with a little more
marinade while cooking the steaks. Brush the sides with oils
then turn the steaks over and cook for 3-6 minutes on the
second side, again basting with the remaining marinade. Season
generously with pepper and sprinkle on some coarsely ground
sea salt just before serving.

■ COOK'S TIP

After reducing the
marinade, add a few
tablespoons of double
cream and heat gently until
thickened to make a lovely
rich sauce.

118 BEEF, GINGER AND SOY KEBABS

Preparation time:
15 minutes, plus
marinating

Cooking time:
4-8 minutes

Serves 4

Calories:
926 per portion

YOU WILL NEED:
1 kg/2 lb sirloin steak, trimmed of
  all fat and cut into 2 cm/¾ inch
  cubes
1 x 5 cm/2 inch piece fresh root
  ginger, very finely sliced
100 ml/3½ fl oz soy sauce
100 ml/3½ fl oz saki or dry sherry
85 ml/3 fl oz peanut or sunflower
  oil
10 spring onions, green tops only,
  finely chopped

Thread the cubed beef and the ginger slices on to long, thin
skewers, placing a slice of ginger after two or three meat cubes.
Lay the skewers in a long dish or roasting tin.

Mix together the soy sauce, saki and oil, then pour the
marinade over the meat. Turn the skewers two or three times,
then cover and leave in a cool place to marinate for at least 8
hours. Remove the skewers from the marinade and pour the
marinade into a small jug.

Grill the kebabs over very hot coals for 4 minutes for rare,
6 minutes for medium, or 8 minutes for well done. Turn once
half-way through the cooking time and brush with the
marinade every minute or so.

Sprinkle some chopped spring onions tops on to four
individual plates then push the meat off the skewers on to the
onion tops. Serve immediately with rice.

■ COOK'S TIP

The slivers of ginger must
be very thinly sliced or they
will be too hot for even the
bravest of palates! The
easiest way to do this is to
cut the ginger into three

pieces and then slice it with
the grain. For a milder
ginger flavour, dice the
ginger finely and add to the
marinade.

119 PAPRIKA BURGERS

Preparation time:	YOU WILL NEED:
15 minutes, plus chilling	1 onion, finely chopped
	675 g/1½ lb lean minced beef
	1 green pepper, seeded and finely chopped
Cooking time:	2 spring onions, finely chopped
4-12 minutes	1 tablespoon tomato purée
	1 teaspoon paprika
Serves 6	3 teaspoons salt
	½ teaspoon pepper
Calories:	green pepper slices, to garnish
245 per portion	

Place all the ingredients in a large bowl and mix thoroughly. Divide the mixture into six and pat each piece firmly into a neat round shape about 1 cm/½ inch thick. Chill for 1 hour.

Grill the burgers over hot coals: for rare burgers allow 2 minutes each side; for medium, 4 minutes and for well-done, 6 minutes each side.

Serve with toasted bread rolls and relishes.

120 VEAL CHOPS WITH ROQUEFORT AND MUSHROOM STUFFING

Preparation time:	YOU WILL NEED:
15 minutes	4 veal chops
	1 tablespoon olive oil
Cooking time:	FOR THE STUFFING
35-40 minutes	75 g/3 oz bacon rashers
	100 g/4 oz button mushrooms, sliced
Serves 4	1 onion, chopped
	50 g/2 oz Roquefort cheese, crumbled
Calories:	50 g/2 oz parsley, chopped
256 per portion	salt and pepper

First prepare the stuffing. Cut the bacon into small dice and place in a saucepan. Heat gently until the fat runs, then add the mushrooms, onion and a little oil if the mixture seems too dry. Cook for 2-3 minutes. Remove from the heat, allow to cool slightly, then mix in the cheese, parsley and seasoning to taste.

Make a slit in each chop and fill with stuffing. Brush both sides of the chops with the oil, then secure each slit with wooden toothpicks or cocktail sticks.

Place the meat on the grid and cook over medium coals for 30 minutes, turning once. Remove the cocktail sticks before serving with a crisp salad and crusty bread.

■ COOK'S TIP

Make the Paprika Burgers, omitting the paprika and pepper and adding 2 teaspoons Worcestershire sauce and 1 teaspoon French mustard. Coat the chilled burgers with coarsely ground black pepper and serve with sliced tomato.

■ COOK'S TIP

Although Roquefort is the ideal cheese to use, it can be replaced by a less expensive blue cheese, such as Stilton.

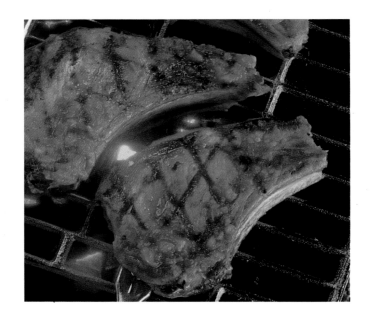

121 PORK CHOPS PROVENCALE

Preparation time:
15 minutes

Cooking time:
about 25 minutes

Serves 6

Calories:
132 per portion

YOU WILL NEED:
4 pork loin chops
FOR THE SAUCE
225 g/8 oz canned tomatoes
1 small onion, finely chopped
2 tablespoons white wine
1 tablespoon tomato purée
1 teaspoon paprika
1 teaspoon dried 'herbes de
    Provence'
1 teaspoon oil

First make the sauce: drain the tomatoes, reserving the liquid. Chop the tomatoes and combine with the remaining sauce ingredients in a bowl. Stir in about 2 tablespoons of the reserved tomato liquid.

Brush the chops on both sides with the sauce and arrange on the greased grid. Grill over hot coals for about 25 minutes, turning occasionally and brushing with more of the sauce until cooked through.

Heat the remaining sauce and serve with the barbecued chops and a salad.

122 SWEET-AND-SOUR PORK KEBABS

Preparation time:
15 minutes

Cooking time:
15-17 minutes

Makes 8-9 kebabs

Calories:
114 per portion

YOU WILL NEED:
200 g/7 oz canned pineapple cubes
    in syrup
1 green pepper
1 red pepper
450 g/1 lb lean pork fillet, cubed
1 tablespoon tomato purée
2 tablespoons brown sugar
2 tablespoons vinegar
2 teaspoons Worcestershire sauce
pinch chilli seasoning
salt and pepper
2 teaspoons cornflour

Drain the pineapple syrup into a small pan. Cut the peppers into 2.5-cm/1-inch squares, discarding the core and seeds. Thread the pork, pineapple and peppers alternately on to metal skewers.

Stir the tomato purée, sugar, vinegar, Worcestershire sauce, chilli seasoning and good shake of salt and pepper into the pineapple syrup. Bring to the boil. Mix the cornflour with 1 tablespoon of cold water and stir into the boiling sauce. Cook for 1 minute. Brush the sauce over the kebabs.

Grill the kebabs over hot coals for 10-12 minutes, turning and brushing frequently with the sauce. Serve the remaining sauce separately.

■ COOK'S TIP

'Herbes de Provence' is a mixture of herbs including thyme, marjoram, oregano, basil and sometimes savory, all of which grow in the South of France.

■ COOK'S TIP

Pork goes bad quickly in hot weather, so it should be kept in the refrigerator and only brought to room temperature just before it is barbecued. Frozen pork must first be thoroughly thawed.

123 GREEK SOUVLAKI

Preparation time:	YOU WILL NEED:
20 minutes, plus	1 kg/2 lb belly pork, boned
marinating	2 onions
	1 garlic clove
Cooking time:	2 bay leaves
15-20 minutes	150 ml/¼ pint dry white wine
	6 tablespoons oil
Serves 8	½ teaspoon ground cumin
	½ teaspoon ground coriander
Calories:	½ teaspoon ground cinnamon
269 per portion	½ teaspoon ground cardamom
	salt and pepper
	extra bay leaves

Cut the belly pork into 2.5-cm/1-inch cubes. Peel and finely chop one onion and the garlic; quarter the other onion. Place in a bowl with all the other ingredients except the extra bay leaves; mix together and add the pork. Marinate for at least 4 hours.

Thread the meat, quartered onion and extra bay leaves on to skewers and grill over hot coals for 15-20 minutes, turning frequently and basting with the marinade.

Serve with lemon slices, shredded cabbage and carrot.

124 PORK CHOPS WITH CAPER AND GHERKIN MARINADE

Preparation time:	YOU WILL NEED:
15 minutes, plus	4 sparerib chops
marinating	1 bay leaf
	2 tablespoons capers
Cooking time:	2 gherkins, chopped
32-44 minutes	4 tablespoons dry white wine or
	cider
Serves 4	2 teaspoons caster sugar
	2 tablespoons olive, sunflower or
Calories:	soya oil
304 per portion	½ teaspoon French mustard

Place the sparerib chops in a large, shallow dish with the bay leaf. Scatter the capers and gherkins over the top. Mix the wine or cider, sugar, oil and mustard and pour over. Leave for 2 hours to marinate.

Drain the chops and grill them over hot coals for 6-7 minutes on each side. Move the chops to warm coals and continue cooking for a further 10-15 minutes, basting frequently with the marinade. Cook until the juices run clear when meat is pierced with a skewer. Serve with grilled onion rings.

■ COOK'S TIP

If you do not have all the spices for this recipe, use 2 teaspoons garam masala instead (from Indian stores). Use Greek Retsina or Domestica wine and *drink the remainder with the meal for a truly Greek flavour.*

■ COOK'S TIP

Sparerib chops are quite meaty, and capers and gherkins give them a piquant flavour. Serve any remaining marinade with the meat.

125 CHILLI PORK

Preparation time:	YOU WILL NEED:
20 minutes, plus	*1 small green pepper*
marinating	*2 small green chillies*
	1 garlic clove
Cooking time:	*4 tomatoes*
16-20 minutes	*1 small onion*
	4 tablespoons medium-sweet
Serves 6	*white wine*
	salt and pepper
Calories:	*6 boned pork chump chops*
198 per portion	

Cut the green pepper and chillies in half, discarding core and seeds. Peel the garlic. Skin and seed the tomatoes. Peel the onion. Place all the vegetables, wine and a good shake of salt and pepper into a food processor or liquidizer and blend to a paste. Place the chops in a shallow dish and spread with the pepper mixture, cover and leave to marinate for 2 hours.

Remove the meat and drain off the marinade and heat in a small pan.

Sear the chops over hot coals for 3-4 minutes on each side. Move to warm coals and cook for a further 10-12 minutes, or until the meat is firm and golden brown. Serve each chop with a little of the marinade.

126 BARBECUED FILLET

Preparation time:	YOU WILL NEED:
25 minutes	*500 g/1¼ lb pork tenderloin*
	fillet, cubed
Cooking time:	*1 green pepper, cored, seeded and*
about 25 minutes	*cut into squares*
	200 g/7 oz canned pineapple
Serves 4	*chunks, drained*
	Oriental Marinade (see Cook's Tip)
Calories:	*4 tomatoes*
280 per portion	

Put the pork, green pepper and pineapple in a shallow dish. Pour over the Oriental Marinade and turn to coat. Leave to marinate in the refrigerator for 2 hours.

Thread the pork, green pepper and pineapple alternately on to skewers, leaving space for a whole tomato at the end. Grill over medium-hot coals for about 20 minutes, turning occasionally and brushing with the marinade from time to time. Place the tomatoes on the ends of the skewers for the last 5 minutes.

Serve with rice, a green salad and sweet and sour sauce.

■ COOK'S TIP

Be very careful not to touch your face or eyes with your fingers when preparing the chillies as the juice burns. Wash your hands immediately afterwards.

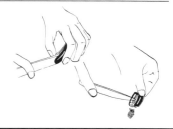

■ COOK'S TIP

For Oriental marinade, mix together 4 tablespoons each soy sauce and sherry, 2 tablespoons clear honey, 1 teaspoon ground cinnamon, pepper, ½ teaspoon ground *cloves, 4 tablespoons cold tea and 1 crushed garlic clove.*

127 PICNIC MEAT LOAF

Preparation time:
15 minutes

Cooking time:
1 hour, plus
standing

Oven temperature:
180 C/350 F/gas 4

Serves 4

Calories:
318 per portion

YOU WILL NEED:
225 g/8 oz minced beef
350 g/12 oz minced pork
50 g/2 oz fresh wholemeal
    breadcrumbs
1 tablespoon chopped fresh herbs
1 tablespoon Worcestershire sauce
1 tablespoon tomato ketchup
1 onion, finely chopped
1 garlic clove, crushed
salt and pepper
1 egg, beaten

Grease a 1-kg/2-lb loaf tin.

Place all the ingredients except the egg in a large bowl and stir well to mix. Stir the beaten egg into the mixture to bind then spoon into the greased tin.

Cover the meat loaf with foil and bake in the preheated oven for 1 hour, until firm.

Remove the loaf from the oven and leave to stand for 5 minutes. Pour off the excess fat and leave until cold.

Transport the meat loaf to the picnic wrapped in a double thickness of foil.

128 STILTON-TOPPED BACON STEAKS

Preparation time:
25 minutes, plus
chilling

Cooking time:
about 20 minutes

Serves 4

Calories:
404 per portion

YOU WILL NEED:
75 g/3 oz butter, softened
75 g/3 oz Stilton cheese, crumbled
salt and pepper
6 spring onions, trimmed
pared rind and juice of 2 oranges
4 bacon steaks, about 150 g/5 oz
    each
oil
parsley sprigs, to garnish

First make the Stilton cheese butter: beat together the butter and cheese and season with salt and pepper to taste. Place on a sheet of foil and form into a roll. Chill until firm.

Slice the onions and cut the orange rind into fine shreds. Stir both into the orange juice and set aside.

Snip the fat off the steaks at regular intervals to keep them flat during cooking. Brush on both sides with oil. Place in a large pan or on an old baking sheet. Cook over hot coals for 10 minutes. Turn the steaks, spoon over the orange juice and onion mixture and continue cooking for a further 10 minutes, or until the bacon is tender.

Cut the cheese butter into four slices. Serve each steak garnished with a slice of orange, a slice of cheese butter and a sprig of parsley.

■ COOK'S TIP

Eating outdoors creates hearty appetites, so rather than possibly keeping guests waiting too long to be fed, it is a good idea to make a meat loaf in advance and serve it as an appetizer with salad.

■ COOK'S TIP

Should the fire not be entirely burnt out when the cooking is finished, douse the charcoal with a little water and save it for your next barbecue.

129 ONION-SMOTHERED CHOPS

Preparation time:
10 minutes, plus
chilling

Cooking time:
about 30 minutes

Serves 6

Calories:
199 per portion

YOU WILL NEED:
6 unsmoked bacon chops
300 ml/½ pint beer
pepper
1 bay leaf
3 onions, sliced
2 tablespoons black treacle
1 tablespoon lemon juice
2 tablespoons oil

Put the chops in a shallow dish and pour the beer over.
Sprinkle with pepper, add the bay leaf and a third of the onion
slices. Chill for at least 8 hours. Then drain the marinade into
a pan and boil until reduced by half. Stir in the treacle and
lemon juice.

Heat the oil and use to fry the remaining onion slices until
they begin to soften. Set aside.

Arrange the bacon chops on the greased grid. Grill over hot
coals for 10 minutes, brushing frequently with the beer baste.
Turn the chops, brush again, top with fried onion rings and
spoon over more of the baste. Cook for a further 10 minutes,
or until the chops are tender and glazed. Serve with a tomato
salad and baked potatoes.

130 BACON-WRAPPED SAUSAGES

Preparation time:
5 minutes

Cooking time:
20 minutes

Serves 4

Calories:
441 per portion

YOU WILL NEED:
450 g/1 lb pork sausages
100 g/4 oz Cheddar cheese, sliced
8 bacon rashers
4 teaspoons French mustard

Cook the sausages over medium coals for about 15 minutes,
then slit them lengthways, almost through. Fill with the cheese
slices and press the sausages together again.

Spread the bacon rashers with mustard and wrap around
the sausages, securing the ends with wooden cocktail sticks.
Place them on the grill again and cook over medium coals for a
further 5 minutes, or until the cheese melts and the bacon is
crisp. Serve with a mixed green salad and potato crisps.

▨ COOK'S TIP

*Keep a plastic sprinkler
bottle filled with water
nearby to douse the flames
when the food flares from
dripping fat. Do not use a
bottle that previously*
*contained inflammable
liquids.*

▨ COOK'S TIP

*Remember to provide
plenty of paper napkins and
some finger bowls as eating
barbecued food can become
rather messy.*

131 LIVER WITH LEMON, SAGE AND BLACK PEPPER

Preparation time:	YOU WILL NEED:
10 minutes	*450 g/1 lb lamb's liver, thinly sliced*
	3 tablespoons lemon juice
Cooking time:	*salt and pepper*
about 12 minutes	*2 fresh sage sprigs (or ¼ teaspoon*
	dried sage)
Serves 6	*2 tablespoons oil*
	2 tablespoons butter, melted
Calories:	
194 per portion	

Brush the liver liberally with lemon juice; sprinkle with a little salt and a lot of pepper. Chop the sage very finely and add to the oil and butter; brush the mixture over the liver.

Grill the liver over medium-hot coals for 6 minutes on each side, brushing well with oil and butter. Test with a skewer; the meat juices will run clear when the liver is cooked. Serve with rice and a mixed salad.

132 APPLE AND RAISIN STUFFED BACON CHOPS

Preparation time:	YOU WILL NEED:
10 minutes	*1 large cooking apple*
	knob of butter
Cooking time:	*25 g/1 oz raisins*
15-20 minutes	*oil*
	4 thick bacon chops
Serves 4	
Calories:	
461 per portion	

Peel, core and slice the apple. Place it in a small pan with the butter and cook over a low heat until the apples are tender. Break up with a fork and add the raisins.

Using a sharp knife, cut into the side of the chop to make a pocket but do not cut all the way through the bacon. Pack the apple and raisin mixture inside the chops.

Brush the chops with oil and grill over medium coals for 6-8 minutes on each side or until the meat feels firm.

■ COOK'S TIP

Lamb's liver, kidneys or heart, calves' liver or kidney's, or pig's kidneys are ideal offal to grill. Barbecuing seals the outside, allowing the inside to stay juicy and tender. The pieces should be thin enough to cook quickly, but not so thin that they will overcook and dry out.

■ COOK'S TIP

Bacon chops are thickly cut, lean back-rashers. These don't take too long to cook. Choose thick ones so that you can make a pocket for the stuffing.

133 DEVILLED GAMMON WITH PINEAPPLE

Preparation time:
5 minutes

Cooking time:
7-9 minutes

Serves 4

Calories:
467 per portion

YOU WILL NEED:
4 gammon steaks, smoked or
    unsmoked, about 175 g/
    6 oz each
melted butter
2 teaspoons English or French
    mustard
2 tablespoons demerara sugar
1 small can pineapple rings

Snip the rind around the gammon steaks to prevent them curling up. Brush each steak with melted butter, spread thickly with mustard and sprinkle with sugar.

Grill the gammon steaks over medium-hot coals for 3-4 minutes on each side.

Drain the pineapple rings, grill them for 1 minute on each side, then place on top of the gammon. Serve with potato salad.

134 SAUSAGES BASTED WITH BEER

Preparation time:
5 minutes, plus
marinating

Cooking time:
30 minutes

Serves 6-8

Calories:
528 - 396 per portion

YOU WILL NEED:
1.5 kg/3 lb good quality pork
    sausages
FOR THE BEER MARINADE
300 ml/½ pint brown ale
2 garlic cloves, crushed
½ tablespoon allspice berries,
    ground
1 x 2.5 cm/1 inch piece orange rind

First, make the marinade: stir the beer, garlic and allspice berries together, then add the piece of orange rind.

Prick the sausages all over with a fine fork, then lay them in a shallow glass dish. Pour the marinade over, cover and leave to marinate for 4 hours, turning them half way through.

Drain the marinade into a jug, then grill the sausages on a greased grid over hot calls for about 30 minutes, constantly turning and basting with the marinade.

Serve in soft baps with a whole-grain mustard.

■ COOK'S TIP

Keep portable metal barbecues under cover when not in use or they will rust. Remember to scrape down and clean the grid frequently for best results.

■ COOK'S TIP

Beer makes a delicious and simple basting sauce. If liked, wrap the baps in foil and warm on the side of the barbecue.

135 SAUSAGE AND KIDNEY KEBABS

Preparation time:	YOU WILL NEED:
15 minutes	6 lamb's kidneys
	350 g/12 oz pork cocktail or
Cooking time:	chipolata sausages
20 minutes	400 g/14 oz canned pineapple
	chunks in natural juice
Serves 6	6 bay leaves
	FOR THE BASTE
Calories:	3 tablespoons pineapple juice
162 per portion	from the can
	2 tablespoons white wine
	1 tablespoon clear honey
	1 teaspoon dried mixed herbs

Place the kidneys in a bowl and pour boiling water over them. Leave for 1 minute, drain and pour cold water over. Drain again; skin and quarter the kidneys and snip out the cores.

If using chipolata sausages, twist these in half to make about eighteen smaller sausages. Drain the pineapple chunks, reserving the juice. Thread the kidney, sausages, pineapple and bay leaves on to six oiled skewers.

Combine all the ingredients for the baste and use to brush the kebabs. Place the kebabs on a greased and grill over hot coals for about 20 minutes, turning the skewers frequently and brushing with the baste, until the sausages are cooked. Serve with French bread and a rice salad.

136 CUMBERLAND SAUSAGE GRILL

Preparation time:	YOU WILL NEED:
2 minutes	1 Cumberland sausage
	oil
Cooking time:	
15-20 minutes	
Serves 6	
Calories:	
353 per portion	

Insert two metal skewers through the sausage to prevent it uncurling, brush it with oil and grill over hot coals for 15-20 minutes, turning frequently to prevent the skin from bursting or burning.

Remove the skewers and slice the sausage to serve.
Serve with potato salad and crusty bread.

COOK'S TIP

Cover brick barbecues to keep out rainwater and remove the metal parts. A dustbin lid will do but ensure it is well anchored or it may blow away.

COOK'S TIP

A Cumberland sausage is made from coarsely ground pork, well seasoned with nutmeg and pepper. It can contain as much as 98% pork but recipes vary between butchers and cereal is often added.

VEGETABLES

Vegetables, served warm or cold, are essential elements in summer cooking. Recipes in this chapter include many for cooking on the barbecue and many more that can be easily packed for taking on picnics. While there are plenty to choose for serving as accompaniments for main meal dishes, there are also vegetable recipes here that make ideal starters or light meals on their own.

137 THREE PEPPER KEBABS

Preparation time:
15 minutes

Cooking time:
7-10 minutes

Serves 4

Calories:
332 per portion

YOU WILL NEED:
2 green peppers, seeded and
    chopped into 2.5 cm/1 inch
    squares
2 medium red peppers, seeded and
    chopped into 2.5 cm/1 inch
    squares
2 medium yellow peppers, seeded
    and chopped into 2.5 cm/1 inch
    squares
about 120 ml/4 fl oz olive oil
2 garlic cloves, finely chopped
coarsely ground sea salt
1 tablespoon crushed black
    peppercorns
3 tablespoons lemon juice

Thread the peppers on to 8 bamboo skewers. A medium pepper will normally give about 12-16 pieces so there should be about 3-4 pieces of each colour pepper on each skewer. Alternate the colours as you thread them.

Brush the peppers generously on all sides with the oil and cook on the greased grill of a preheated barbecue for 7-10 minutes, turning and basting with oil every 1-2 minutes. When they are just beginning to char they are done. Baste again with olive oil.

Put the skewers on serving plates, then sprinkle each one with a little of the finely chopped garlic, generously season with salt and pepper and then pour over some lemon juice.

■ COOK'S TIP

It is not necessary to peel the peppers as the skin gives a pleasant crunchy texture. If you prefer skinned peppers char them first under a grill until the skin *blackens and blisters, then peel off the skin. Watch them carefully during barbecuing.*

138 BUTTON MUSHROOMS IN VINE LEAVES

Preparation time:
40 minutes, plus soaking

Cooking time:
5 minutes

Serves 4

Calories:
350 per portion

YOU WILL NEED:
20 medium button mushrooms
24 vine leaves
about 150 ml/¼ pint olive oil
2 large garlic cloves, finely chopped
3 tablespoons finely chopped fresh
    parsley
salt and pepper

Wipe the mushrooms with a damp cloth and trim the stalks. Prepare the vine leaves (see recipe 44). Four extra leaves are allowed for in case of tearing. Spear each mushroom with a bamboo skewer and dip it into the oil, leave for a couple of seconds to absorb the oil, then remove and shake off the excess. Place the mushrooms, stalk side up, on a plate.

Press 2-3 small pieces of garlic into the stalk or stalk cavity of each mushroom, then sprinkle with a little parsley, pressing it down with the back of a spoon. Season well.

Place the vine leaves on a flat surface, vein side up, and brush each one with a little oil, then place a mushroom in the centre of each leaf. Carefully fold over the portion of the leaf to the left of the stem, then the right, then the sides and finally cover the mushroom with the top of the leaf. Brush the parcels with oil and put on a plate, rounded side upwards.

Cook the wrapped mushrooms in a greased hinged grill on a barbecue for 5 minutes, turning after 2½ minutes.

■ COOK'S TIP

Serve the mushrooms very hot in the vine leaves. Guests can either remove the vine leaves to eat them or eat them in the crispy wrappings.

139 GRILLED BABY SWEETCORN

Preparation time:
15 minutes

Cooking time:
6-7 minutes

Serves 4-6

Calories:
278 - 185 per portion

YOU WILL NEED:
450 g/1 lb baby sweetcorn
salt and pepper
100 g/4 oz butter
1 tablespoon lemon juice
1 garlic clove, crushed

Rub the sweetcorn generously with salt and pepper, then thread on to skewers.

Put the butter, lemon juice and garlic into a heavy-based saucepan and heat until bubbling and melted. Do this in the kitchen or over the barbecue. Once the butter is melted the saucepan should be put at the edge of the coals so that it keeps warm but does not burn.

Brush the corn with some of the melted butter mixture then cook on the greased grill of a preheated barbecue for 6-7 minutes, turning them every minute or so and constantly brushing with the butter.

When they begin to turn golden-brown, push the corn off the skewers into a warmed serving dish and pour over any remaining melted butter mixture.

140 GARLIC-STUFFED MUSHROOMS

Preparation time:
20 minutes, plus
marinating

Cooking time:
14-16 minutes

Serves 6

Calories:
126 per portion

YOU WILL NEED:
2 tablespoons olive oil
2 tablespoons lemon juice
salt and pepper
6 large round mushroom caps
1 large onion
2 garlic cloves
50 g/2 oz butter
50 g/2 oz breadcrumbs
4 tablespoons parsley

Mix the oil, lemon juice and a little salt and pepper together in a large bowl. Add the mushrooms, toss together and leave for 2-3 hours.

Peel and very finely chop the onion. Peel and crush the garlic. Melt the butter in a small pan, and gently fry the onion and garlic for 5 minutes or until the onion is transparent. Remove from the heat. Stir in the breadcrumbs and the chopped parsley.

Drain the mushroom marinade into the breadcrumbs. Mix well then pack the stuffing into the mushroom caps. Place on a tray, cover and leave until ready to cook. Cook over medium-hot coals for 8-10 minutes or until heated through.

COOK'S TIP

For a delicious variation, wrap the corn in derinded smoked streaky bacon, cut into 5-7.5 cm (2-3 inch) lengths, according to the size of the corn. Do not season the corn with salt but sprinkle with black pepper before wrapping, if liked. Cook for about 8-9 minutes until the bacon is crisp.

COOK'S TIP

These are tasty as a vegetable and great as a starter, too. They can be prepared hours in advance and are then quick to cook.

141 STUFFED MUSHROOMS

Preparation time:	YOU WILL NEED:
10 minutes	*8 mushrooms*
	2 tablespoons fresh white
Cooking time:	*breadcrumbs*
about 5 minutes	*1 small onion, finely chopped*
	1 teaspoon mixed dried herbs
Serves 4	*1 tomato, skinned and chopped*
	1 tablespoon oil
Calories:	
48 per portion	

Remove the stalks from the mushrooms and chop them finely. Mix the stalks with the breadcrumbs, onion, herbs and tomato.

Brush the mushroom caps with oil and arrange on an oiled flameproof plate. Spread each cap with the stuffing and place on the barbecue grid to cook.

Decorate with sprigs of parsley, and strips of pimiento or tomato, if liked.

142 PILAFF

Preparation time:	YOU WILL NEED:
10 minutes	*25 g/1 oz butter*
	1 small onion, peeled and finely
Cooking time:	*diced*
20-25 minutes	*175 g/6 oz long-grain rice*
	450 ml/¾ pint stock or water
Oven temperature:	*pinch of powdered saffron or*
180 C/350 F/gas 4	*turmeric*
	½ teaspoon dried oregano
Serves 4	*salt and pepper*
Calories:	
219 per portion	

Melt the butter in a saucepan. Add the onion and cook until soft but not brown. Add the rice and cook for 2 to 3 minutes, then stir in the remaining ingredients with salt and pepper to taste. Simmer gently over a low heat on top of the stove or in a preheated moderate oven until the liquid is absorbed and the rice is fluffy and tender. This pilaff is excellent with all skewered food.

■ COOK'S TIP

Bacon, crisply grilled then chopped into small pieces, will add flavour and 'bite' to the stuffing for these mushrooms.

■ COOK'S TIP

For a green rice, omit saffron (for yellow colouring) and add 2 tablespoons chopped fresh parsley and 1 tablespoon chopped fresh chives.

143 MIXED VEGETABLE PILAFF

Preparation time:
15 minutes

Cooking time:
15 minutes

Serves 4

Calories:
168 per portion

YOU WILL NEED:
100 g/4 oz Basmati rice
350 ml/12 fl oz water
1 tablespoon vegetable oil
1 x 1.25-cm/½-inch piece
   cinnamon stick
2 whole cloves
2 green cardamom pods
6 cashew nuts, halved
6 whole almonds (not blanched)
1 tablespoon sultanas
75 g/3 oz frozen mixed vegetables,
   defrosted
salt

Wash the rice 5 times until the water is clear. Drain well. Place in a heatproof glass casserole, add the water and boil for 5 minutes. Reduce the heat, cover and simmer for 10 minutes.

Meanwhile, heat the oil in a frying pan and use to fry the cinnamon stick, cloves and cardamom for 1 minute. Put in the cashews, almonds and sultanas, stir over the heat for a few seconds then add the mixed vegetables. Sprinkle in a little salt to taste and cook gently for 5 minutes.

Lightly fork the spice mixture into the cooked rice, cover and keep warm.

■ COOK'S TIP

This is a useful barbecue dish, as it can be prepared in advance and kept warm, in a cool oven or on the side of the barbecue, in its heatproof casserole.

144 VEGETABLE KEBABS

Preparation time:
20 minutes, plus standing

Cooking time:
13-15 minutes

Serves 4

Calories:
90 per portion

YOU WILL NEED:
225 g/8 oz aubergine, cut into
   2.5 cm/1 inch cubes
225 g/8 oz courgettes, cut into
   2.5 cm/1 inch cubes
salt
100 g/4 oz button mushrooms
1 small green pepper, cored,
   seeded and cut into 2.5 cm/1
   inch squares
1 small red pepper, cored, seeded
   and cut into 2.5 cm/1 inch
   squares
2 small tomatoes, halved
Barbecue sauce (see recipe 198)

Place the aubergine and courgettes in a colander set over a plate. Sprinkle with salt and leave to stand for about 30 minutes to remove the bitter juices. Rinse under cold running water, then pat dry. Steam the aubergine, courgettes, mushrooms and peppers for 5 minutes or blanch them for 3 minutes in boiling water, then drain.

Allow the vegetables to cool slightly, then thread them on to 4 oiled kebab skewers. Pour the barbecue sauce into a shallow dish and lay the kebabs in it. Spoon the sauce over them and leave for 5 minutes.

Lift the kebabs from the sauce and cook on a hot barbecue for 5 minutes. Place half a tomato on the end of each skewer, then turn the kebabs, brush with the barbecue sauce and cook for a further 5 minutes or until the vegetables are tender.

Serve the remaining barbecue sauce separately.

■ COOK'S TIP

For a more fruity mixture, omit the peppers and mushrooms and use cubes of fresh or canned pineapple, firm apricots or peaches instead.

145 BAKED CORN ON THE COB

Preparation time:
5 minutes

Cooking time:
20-30 minutes

Serves 4

Calories:
223 per portion

YOU WILL NEED:
4 corn cobs, husks and silk
    removed
sugar
salt
4 tablespoons water
50 g/2 oz butter, melted

Place each corn cob on a piece of foil large enough to contain it and sprinkle with a little sugar, salt and 1 tablespoon water.

Seal the edges of the foil firmly, to make parcels.

Cook on a hot barbecue for 20-30 minutes, or until tender. Open out the parcels and pour over the melted butter. Serve straight from the foil.

146 CREAM CHEESE-STUFFED POTATOES

Preparation time:
10 minutes

Cooking time:
40-50 minutes

Serves 4

Calories:
280 per portion

YOU WILL NEED:
4 large potatoes
salt and pepper
100 g/4 oz full fat soft cheese
1 small onion, finely chopped
1 tablespoon snipped chives

Scrub the potatoes in cold water and pat dry with absorbent kitchen paper. Prick the skins all over with a fork and rub well with salt.

Wrap each potato in foil and place amongst the hot coals of the barbecue. Bake for 40-50 minutes, turning frequently, or until the potatoes feel soft when pinched.

Meanwhile, cream together the cheese, onion and chives and season to taste with salt and pepper.

Scoop the flesh from the cooked potatoes and mix with the cream cheese mixture. Pile back into the potato shells and serve.

■ COOK'S TIP

Other vegetables may be successfully cooked in foil on the barbecue. For baked courgettes, allow 1 courgette per person. Parboil for 4 minutes in salted water, then drain and cut into thick slices. Put one sliced courgette on foil, adding a chopped tomato and seasoning before sealing.

■ COOK'S TIP

Reduce the cooking time by parboiling the potatoes for 10 minutes before wrapping them in foil.

147 BARBECUED CHILLI BEANS

Preparation time:
5 minutes

Cooking time:
about 20 minutes

Serves 6

Calories:
121 per portion

YOU WILL NEED:
25 g/1 oz margarine or butter
1 large onion, chopped
4 rashers streaky bacon, rinded
   and chopped
¼ teaspoon chilli powder
1 x 198 g/7 oz can tomatoes
1 x 439 g/15½ oz can baked
   beans
salt and pepper
dash of Worcestershire sauce

Melt the margarine in a saucepan, add the onion and fry gently for 5 minutes until soft and lightly coloured. Add the bacon to the pan and fry for about 8 minutes until crisp and golden.

Stir in the chilli powder, then the tomatoes with their juice and the baked beans. Stir well and simmer gently, either on the stove or on the barbecue, until heated through.

Season with salt, pepper and Worcestershire sauce to taste.

148 AUBERGINE AND CHILLI KEBABS

Preparation time:
15 minutes, plus
salting

Cooking time:
15 minutes

Serves 4

Calories:
291 per portion

YOU WILL NEED:
450 g/1 lb aubergines, cut into
   2.5 cm/1 inch cubes
salt
9 tablespoons olive oil
2-3 green chillies, trimmed, cut
   into fine rings, and seeded
freshly ground black pepper

Place the aubergine cubes in one layer on a flat plate, sprinkle heavily with salt and leave to stand for 30 minutes to draw out the bitter juices.

Rinse the aubergines thoroughly under cold running water, then pat dry with absorbent kitchen paper.

Arrange them on the plate again and brush with half the oil, coating all sides of each piece. Leave for 15 minutes.

Thread the aubergines on to bamboo skewers, alternating every 2-3 pieces with a ring of chilli. Cook on the greased grill of a barbecue for 5 minutes, then baste with the remaining oil and turn and cook for a further 10 minutes until crisp.

■ COOK'S TIP

Children enjoy these beans, though the addition of a little sophistication, in the shape of the chilli powder, makes them good for adults, too. Serve them with barbecued sausages or burgers.

■ COOK'S TIP

These aubergine skewers are delicious but rich, so serve them with a fairly plain meat or fish dish, or even with rice or a pilaff.

149 MANGETOUT WITH LIME BUTTER

Preparation time:
10 minutes, plus
chilling

Cooking time:
6-8 minutes

Serves 6-8

Calories:
227 - 170 per portion

YOU WILL NEED:
100 g/4 oz butter, softened
salt
2 limes
freshly ground black pepper
1 kg/2 lb mangetout, topped
and tailed

Mash the butter well with a little salt in a bowl, then grate the rind of the limes over it. Cut the limes in half and squeeze the juice into the butter; flake a little of the flesh and add that as well. Mix together thoroughly, then season lightly with pepper. Reserve 2 tablespoons of the mixture, then shape the remaining butter into a roll. Wrap in foil and chill for 2 hours.

Bring a large saucepan of salted water to the boil, add the mangetout and cook for 5-7 minutes until al dente. They should still have a crispy bite to them. Drain and refresh under cold water quickly. Return the mangetout to the pan with the reserved lime butter and toss until lightly coated.

Remove the rest of the butter from the refrigerator and cut it into fine slices.

Pile the mangetout into a warmed dish and serve, handing the butter separately. (Each diner should place a knob of butter on the mangetout and let their heat melt it slowly.)

COOK'S TIP

Mangetout, although now widely available, are still a luxury vegetable, so treat them as such. Serve this recipe as a course its own, perhaps with some crusty

French bread to mop up the buttery juices.

150 CHEESE AND POTATO HASH

Preparation time:
15 minutes

Cooking time:
about 20 minutes

Serves 6 - 8

Calories:
277 - 217 per portion

YOU WILL NEED:
1 kg/2 lb potatoes
225 g/8 oz Double Gloucester
cheese
1 onion
salt and pepper

Peel the potatoes and cut them into 1 cm/½ inch cubes. Parboil in salted water for 3 minutes. Drain well. Chop the cheese into 1 cm/½ inch cubes. Peel and finely chop onion. Cut four 30 cm/12 inch squares of foil. Divide the potato, cheese and onion between the pieces of foil; season and make foil parcels, securing the edges tightly. Place over hot coals and cook for 20 minutes until the potato is tender when pierced with a skewer.

COOK'S TIP

Choose a mature cheese to give this dish a good flavour. As well as the Double Gloucester cheese suggested here, try a mature Cheddar.

151 POTATOES LYONNAISE

Preparation time:
10 minutes, plus
cooling

Cooking time:
60-70 minutes

Serves 6-8

Calories:
764 - 573 per portion

YOU WILL NEED:
1 kg/2 lb potatoes
2 large onions
25 g/1 lb butter
3 tablespoons cooking oil
½ teaspoon salt
pepper
1 tablespoon chopped fresh parsley

Peel the potatoes and cook in boiling salted water for 10 minutes. Drain and allow to cool. Cut into thin slices.

Peel and thinly slice the onions. Melt the butter and oil together in a large frying pan; add the onions and fry for 2-3 minutes until they become transparent. Add the potatoes, seasoning and parsley; stir well. Divide the mixture in half and place each on to large squares of double-thickness foil. Bring the edges up together and seal tightly, leaving room for the expansion of steam. Place over hot coals for 45-50 minutes or until the potatoes feel tender when pierced with a skewer.

152 TOMATO AND ONION GRILL

Preparation time:
5 minutes

Cooking time:
about 6 minutes

Serves 6

Calories:
58 per portion

YOU WILL NEED:
2 beef tomatoes
2 large onions
2 tablespoons olive oil
a few sprigs fresh thyme

Slice the tomatoes and onions thickly. Lay them on the base of a hinged wire basket or place on a sheet of foil over the grill-rack. Brush with oil; top with sprigs of thyme and season with salt and pepper. Close the basket and grill over hot coals. Cook for about 3 minutes on each side.

■ COOK'S TIP

*This classic recipe has been
adapted so that it can be
cooked on a barbecue.*

■ COOK'S TIP

*Use large beef tomatoes
which are 'meatier' and
sweeter than the small ones
and will not fall apart. Use
the Spanish onions which
are sweeter, too.*

153 AUBERGINE AND ANCHOVY FANS

Preparation time:
10 minutes

Cooking time:
about 20 minutes

Serves 4

Calories:
147 per portion

YOU WILL NEED:
2 aubergines
4 tomatoes
2 small onions
4 tablespoons cooking oil
2 bay leaves
4 anchovy fillets
salt and pepper
2 bay leaves

Leaving the aubergines whole, and using a sharp knife, cut each one lengthways into slices, taking care not to cut right through the stalk. Brush between each slice with oil and place each aubergine on a double thichness square of foil.

Slice the tomatoes. Peel the onions and cut into wafer-thin slices. Finely chop the anchovy fillets. Divide the tomato, onion and anchovy between each slice of aubergine. Season with salt and pepper and place a bay leaf on each aubergine. Wrap foil around and fold edges tightly. Cook directly on hot coals for 20 minutes or until tender.

154 GRILLED RED PEPPERS

Preparation time:
5 minutes, plus marinating

Cooking time:
5-10 minutes

Serves 4

Calories:
237 per portion

YOU WILL NEED:
4 large red peppers
1 medium onion, finely chopped
6 tablespoons French dressing
  (see Cook's Tip)

Cook the peppers over a hot barbecue grill until the skins begin to blacken. Remove from the grill and peel off the skins. Slice into quarters, removing all seeds and pith.

Mix the peppers and onion together and place in a small dish. Pour the French dressing over the still warm peppers and marinate for 30 minutes before serving with barbecued beef, chops or sausages.

■ COOK'S TIP

These can be prepared in advance Choose small aubergines for this recipe or they will take too long to cook. Half an aubergine is plenty per person!

■ COOK'S TIP

For the French dressing, shake together in a screw-topped jar 2 tablespoons red wine vinegar, 6 tablespoons olive oil, ½ teaspoon salt, ¼ teaspoon *black pepper and 1 crushed garlic clove.*

155 BACON-STUFFED AUBERGINES

Preparation time:
15 minutes, plus
standing

Cooking time:
about 25 minutes

Serves 4

Calories:
177 per portion

YOU WILL NEED:
2 large aubergines
salt and pepper
40 g/1½ oz butter
4 rashers back bacon, chopped
1 medium-sized onion, finely
  chopped
2 large tomatoes, chopped
2 teaspoons chopped thyme
2 teaspoons chopped parsley

Cut the aubergines in half lengthways, scoop out the flesh and chop roughly. Sprinkle the aubergine shells and the chopped flesh with salt and leave to stand for 20 minutes. Rinse well then drain.

Melt the butter in a pan, stir in the chopped aubergine, bacon and onion and cook for 5 minutes, stirring occasionally. Mix in the tomato and herbs and season with salt and pepper to taste. Pile the mixture into the aubergine shells.

Enclose each stuffed aubergine half in a square of foil, shiny side inwards, crimping the edges well together to make airtight parcels. Place the foil parcels on the grid. Barbecue for about 20 minutes, or until the aubergines feel tender when pressed. Fold back the foil to make boat-shaped containers for serving the aubergines.

156 VEGETABLE KEBABS WITH PEANUT SAUCE

Preparation time:
15 minutes, plus
marinating

Cooking time:
about 30 minutes

Serves 4

Calories:
386 per portion

YOU WILL NEED:
3 courgettes, trimmed
3 tablespoons oil
3 tablespoons lemon juice
8 canned baby corn cobs
450 g/1 lb cup mushrooms
8 button onions
2 tomatoes, quartered
FOR THE SAUCE
2 tablespoons oil
1 small onion, chopped
225 g/8 oz flat mushrooms, chopped
100 g/4 oz roast salted peanuts
150 ml/¼ pint water
2 tablespoons soy sauce
few drops of Tabasco sauce
salt and pepper

Cut the courgettes into 2.5-cm/1-inch pieces. Put them with the oil, lemon juice, corn and mushrooms in a bowl, mix lightly and leave to stand for at least 2 hours, stirring occasionally.

For the sauce, heat the oil in a pan and fry the onion and mushrooms for 8 minutes. Transfer to a blender and blend for 30 seconds. Add the peanuts and blend for a further 30 seconds, until fairly smooth, then return to the pan and stir in the water, soy sauce and Tabasco. Simmer for 10 minutes.

Thread the marinated vegetables, onions and tomato wedges on 4 skewers and barbecue for about 10 minutes, turning occasionally. Serve with the sauce handed separately.

■ COOK'S TIP

For foil-wrapped vegetables from the store cupboard, mix together 225 g/8 oz drained canned sweetcorn and 50 g/2 oz chopped canned pineapple. Divide *between 2 sheets of foil, sprinkle with salt, pepper and pineapple syrup, dot with butter. Fold up the foil and barbecue for about 10 minutes.*

■ COOK'S TIP

To use larger onions, quarter them then plunge into boiling water for 2 minutes to blanch and soften them before threading them on skewers.

157 CURRIED VEGETABLE AND NUT BURGERS

Preparation time: 15 minutes	YOU WILL NEED: *100 g/4 oz roast salted peanuts,* *chopped*
Cooking time: 10 minutes	*100 g/4 oz fresh wholemeal* *breadcrumbs*
	50 g/2 oz sweet green pepper, *chopped*
Serves 8	*1 medium-sized onion, chopped*
	100 g/4 oz mushrooms, sliced
Calories: 128 per portion	*1 egg, beaten* *½ teaspoon dried basil* *½ teaspoon dried parsley* *1 tablespoon bottled curry sauce* *50 g/2 oz plain flour, to coat*

Place the peanuts, breadcrumbs, pepper, onion and mushrooms together in a blender or food processor and switch it on briefly. The ingredients should be finely chopped but not liquidized. Transfer to a bowl and add half the egg, the herbs and curry sauce. Mix well.

Divide the mixture into 8 equal portions and shape each into a round flat cake. Coat the burgers in the remaining egg then cover all over in flour.

Arrange the burgers on the greased grid. Barbecue for 10 minutes, turning them carefully half-way through.

158 GLAZED RED CABBAGE AND BEETROOT

Preparation time: 10 minutes, plus standing	YOU WILL NEED: *150 ml/¼ pint red wine vinegar* *150 ml/¼ pint water* *2 tablespoons soft brown sugar*
Cooking time: 10 minutes	*salt and pepper* *500 g/1 ¼ lb red cabbage,* *shredded*
Serves 6-8	*350 g/12 oz cooked beetroot, diced* *1 tablespoon cornflour mixed to a* *paste with water*
Calories: 127 - 95 per portion	*50 g/2 oz butter or margarine*

Put the vinegar, water and brown sugar into a pan. Add salt and pepper and bring to the boil.

Add the cabbage and cook for 3 minutes, then add the beetroot.

Add the cornflour mixture, stirring until the sauce thickens. Remove the pan from the heat and leave covered for at least 15 minutes.

Just before serving, reheat (on the side of the barbecue if there is room), stirring in the butter. Taste and adjust the seasoning.

■ COOK'S TIP

These burgers go well with wholemeal crusty rolls. A rice salad (recipe 165) or Pilaff (recipe 142) would also be good.

■ COOK'S TIP

This crimson-coloured vegetable combination can be prepared an hour or two ahead, making it ideal to serve at a large party where there may be a lot of last-minute cooking to be done. It is very good served with any barbecue meats, poultry or game.

159 MOULDED SPINACH SALAD

Preparation time:
30 minutes, plus chilling

Serves 6

Calories:
331 per portion

YOU WILL NEED:
225 g/8 oz full fat cream cheese
250 ml/8 fl oz milk
3 teaspoons powdered gelatine
  (1 sachet)
1 medium onion, peeled
150 ml/¼ pint French dressing
  (see Cook's Tip)
½ green pepper, cored, seeded
  and chopped
salt and pepper
75 g/3 oz fresh spinach, stems
  removed, finely shredded
FOR THE GARNISH
lettuce leaves
shredded spinach

Beat the cheese with a wooden spoon until smooth.

Pour half the milk into a pan and sprinkle on the gelatine. Leave for a few minutes to soften, then heat gently, stirring constantly until the gelatine dissolves. Remove from the heat, add the remaining milk and cool for one minute, then beat into the cream cheese to make a smooth mixture.

Chop the onion. Stir the French dressing into the creamed mixture, then add the onion, green pepper and salt and pepper. Chill for 20-30 minutes until the consistency of unbeaten egg white, then fold in the spinach.

Rinse a 1 litre/2 pint ring mould with cold water and turn the mixture into it. Cover with cling film and chill until set - at least 4 hours. Turn out on to a wetted platter and garnish.

COOK'S TIP

For this French dressing, mix 2 tablespoons wine, herb or cider vinegar with 6-8 tablespoons olive oil. Season with salt and pepper.

160 RATATOUILLE

Preparation time:
35 minutes, plus standing

Cooking time:
1 hour

Serves 6-8

Calories:
266 - 200 per portion

YOU WILL NEED:
450 g/1 lb aubergines, trimmed
  and cut into 5 mm/¼ inch slices
450 g/1 lb courgettes,
salt
150 ml/¼ pint olive oil
3 garlic cloves, crushed
1 large onion, thinly sliced
1 yellow or green pepper, cored,
  seeded and sliced
1 red pepper, cored, seeded and
  sliced
450 g/1 lb tomatoes, skinned and
  cut into wedges
freshly ground black pepper
3-4 teaspoons fresh herbs, lightly
  chopped

Put the aubergine and courgette slices on separate plates, sprinkle with salt and leave for 30 minutes to draw the juices.

Heat 4 tablespoons of the oil in a frying pan. Add the garlic and onion and cook until soft and transparent. Add the sliced peppers to the pan. Cook for 5 minutes, then turn the mixture into a large, flameproof casserole.

Rinse and drain the aubergine and courgette slices and pat dry. Set the courgettes aside. Fry the aubergine in a little more oil in batches until lightly browned. Transfer to the casserole. Cook the courgettes in the last of the oil. When almost cooked add the tomatoes. Turn into the casserole. Season, add the herbs and cook over low heat for about 30 minutes until the vegetables are tender but still retain their shape.

COOK'S TIP

As a different way of serving, spoon some ratatouille into small ovenproof dishes and make a hollow with the back of a spoon. Drop in a fresh egg and bake in a preheated hot oven (200 C/400 F/gas 6) for 15-20 minutes.

SALADS

Warm weather meals, whether indoors or outside round a barbecue or picnic hamper, demand salads of all kinds. Here is an excitingly varied selection, including such classics as Tabbouleh and Potato salad and exotics like Goi tom from Vietnam, as well as plenty to please children and adults alike.

161 SALADE NICOISE

Preparation time:
15-20 minutes

Serves 4

Calories:
326 per portion

YOU WILL NEED:
1 firm round lettuce
3 firm tomatoes (skinned if preferred), quartered
2 hard-boiled eggs, quartered
6 anchovy fillets, halved lengthways
12 black olives
2 teaspoons capers
1 x 200 g/7 oz can tuna fish in oil, drained
1 medium red pepper, cored, seeded and cut into strips
6 tablespoons good quality green olive oil
1 large garlic clove, peeled and crushed
salt and pepper
1 tablespoon chopped fresh tarragon

Keep the lettuce whole, wash it well and shake dry. Remove the outer leaves and arrange them around the edge of a salad bowl; cut the remaining lettuce heart into quarters and place in the middle of the bowl.

Add the tomatoes, hard-boiled eggs, anchovy fillets, black olives, capers, tuna fish in chunks, and the strips of pepper.

Mix the oil with the garlic, salt and pepper to taste, and the chopped tarragon. Spoon the dressing evenly over the salad, and toss lightly before serving.

■ COOK'S TIP

If you prefer a slightly tart taste in salad dressing, add a little lemon juice or wine vinegar to the oil, garlic, seasoning and tarragon before spooning the mixture over the salad. Use French, not Russian tarragon: the flavour is far better.

162 RED CABBAGE AND PINEAPPLE COLESLAW

Preparation time:
10 minutes

Serves 4

Calories:
122 per portion

YOU WILL NEED:
1 x 227 g/8 oz can pineapple rings, drained, syrup reserved
6 spring onions, sliced
25 g/1 oz sultanas
175 g/6 oz red cabbage, shredded
2 tablespoons French dressing
salt and pepper
2 chopped spring onions, to garnish

Reserve 1 pineapple ring for the garnish. Chop the remainder and place in a salad bowl with the spring onions, sultanas and cabbage.

Mix 1 tablespoon of the reserved pineapple syrup with the French dressing, season to taste with salt and pepper and add to the salad ingredients.

Toss well and serve garnished with the pineapple ring and chopped spring onions.

■ COOK'S TIP

Not keen on spring onions? Omit them and use 2 chopped celery stalks and 1 tablespoon coarsely chopped walnuts instead.

163 GREEK SALAD

Preparation time:	YOU WILL NEED:
10 minutes	1 Cos lettuce, shredded
	½ cucumber, cut into chunks
Serves 4-6	225 g/8 oz feta cheese, cut into cubes
	4 tomatoes, skinned and sliced
Calories:	6 anchovy fillets, finely chopped
316 - 211 per portion	6 large black olives, halved and stoned
	large pinch of dried marjoram
	1 tablespoon finely chopped parsley
	freshly ground black pepper
	FOR THE DRESSING
	4 tablespoons olive oil
	4 teaspoons white wine vinegar
	1 tablespoon finely chopped fresh mixed herbs
	4 spring onions, chopped
	1 teaspoon sugar
	salt and pepper

Place the shredded lettuce on a serving platter and arrange the cucumber, feta cheese, tomatoes, anchovies and olives on top. Sprinkle with the marjoram, parsley and plenty of black pepper.

Place all the dressing ingredients in a screw-topped jar and shake well. Pour evenly over the salad and serve.

164 COTTAGE SALAD

Preparation time:	YOU WILL NEED:
10 minutes	1 Webb's lettuce or endive
	6 young sorrel leaves, centre stem removed
Serves 6-8	4 dandelion leaves
	handful of rocket, if available
Calories:	bunch of watercress
171 - 129 per portion	handful of borage flowers, violets, chickweed or nasturtium flowers
	25 g/1 oz desiccated coconut, toasted (optional)
	FOR THE DRESSING
	2 tablespoons cider vinegar
	1 teaspoon dry mustard
	1 teaspoon sugar (optional)
	6 tablespoons peanut oil
	salt and pepper

Tear the lettuce or endive by hand into manageable pieces.

Blend the vinegar, mustard and sugar together. Stir in the oil and salt and pepper.

Put all the salad ingredients into an attractive bowl, add the dressing and toss. Garnish the completed salad with the fresh flowers or the toasted coconut.

COOK'S TIP

This salad goes well with kebabs or barbecued leg of lamb. If feta cheese is not available, use Wensleydale, Lancashire or Caerphilly instead.

COOK'S TIP

This dressing is best for green and simple salads where it adds a gloss to the leaves. Olive oil lends distinctive flavour to the dressing. Other oils to use include peanut, sunflower, walnut, hazelnut or grapeseed oil.

165 RICE SALAD

Preparation time:
10 minutes

Cooking time:
10-15 minutes

Serves 4

Calories:
519 per portion

YOU WILL NEED:
225 g/8 oz long-grain rice
12 whole cardamom pods
salt
1 x 227 g/8 oz can pineapple rings,
    drained and roughly chopped
½ cucumber, peeled and diced
50 g/2 oz hazelnuts, roasted and
    skinned
a little paprika, to finish
FOR THE DRESSING
finely grated rind and juice of 1
    orange
6 tablespoons vegetable oil
2 teaspoons curry paste

Cook the rice with the cardamom pods in a saucepan of boiling salted water for 10-15 minutes or until the rice is just tender. Drain the rice and rinse in cold water. Remove the cardamom pods and place the rice in a rigid polythene lidded bowl.

Add the chopped pineapple, cucumber and hazelnuts; stir well to mix.

Place all the dressing ingredients in a screw-topped jar and shake to mix thoroughly. Pour the dressing over the rice salad and fork through evenly. Sprinkle a little paprika over the top.

166 PRAWN, GRAPE AND COTTAGE CHEESE SALAD

Preparation time:
10 minutes

Serves 4

Calories:
282 per portion

YOU WILL NEED:
1 head chicory
350 g/12 oz cottage cheese
100 g/4 oz green grapes, seeded
225 g/8 oz peeled prawns
salt and pepper
4 tablespoons thick mayonnaise
4 tablespoons lemon juice
2 tablespoons finely chopped fresh
    parsley
lemon slices, to garnish

Separate the chicory leaves and use to line the base of a salad bowl. Mix the cottage cheese with the grapes and prawns and season to taste with salt and pepper. Carefully pile the mixture into the centre of the bowl over the chicory leaves.

Combine the mayonnaise, lemon juice and parsley and spoon evenly over the cottage cheese. Garnish the salad before serving with lemon slices.

■ COOK'S TIP

Cardamom, a plant of the ginger family, is native to India, where it is used in many recipes. Green cardamom pods have a more aromatic flavour than the white, sun-bleached pods.

■ COOK'S TIP

Try including melon in this salad. Add ½ small melon cut into cubes or balls to the cottage cheese with the grapes.

167 CURRIED PASTA SALAD

Preparation time:
15 minutes, plus
cooling

Cooking time:
12-15 minutes

Serves 4

Calories:
665 per portion

YOU WILL NEED:
225 g/8 oz pasta shapes
1 small onion, finely chopped
4 tablespoons dry white vermouth
150 ml/¼ pint mayonnaise
2 tablespoons mild curry paste
2 tablespoons apricot jam
2 tablespoons lemon juice
4 large sausages, cooked and
    thinly sliced
FOR THE GARNISH
2 tomatoes, sliced
a few black olives, stoned

Cook the pasta in a saucepan of boiling salted water for 12-15 minutes or until just tender. Drain well and leave to cool.

Meanwhile, place the onion and vermouth in a saucepan and bring to the boil. Simmer for 3 minutes. Remove from the heat and leave to cool.

Stir the mayonnaise, curry paste, apricot jam and lemon juice into the onion mixture. Pour over the pasta: toss to coat evenly. Fold in the sliced sausages.

Turn the mixture into a rigid lidded bowl for easy transport. Garnish with the tomato slices and black olives before serving.

■ COOK'S TIP

This salad makes a good picnic main dish. Serve it with a green salad and French bread.

168 FOUR SEASONS PASTA SALAD

Preparation time:
15-20 minutes

Cooking time:
15-20 minutes

Serves 6

Calories:
300 per portion

YOU WILL NEED:
225 g/8 oz pasta twists
1 head broccoli or ¼ cauliflower,
    divided into small florets
1 red pepper, cored, seeded and
    cut into small strips
1 x 350 g/12 oz can pineapple
    pieces or rings, drained and cut
    into bite-sized pieces
100 g/4 oz cooked ham in one
    slice, diced
FOR THE DRESSING
25 g/1 oz fresh coriander, or a
    mixture of parsley and mint
4 tablespoons grapeseed oil
1 tablespoon white wine vinegar
salt and pepper

Cook the pasta in salted boiling water. Drain, rinse thoroughly.

Slice the broccoli or cauliflower stem finely and separate the florets. Cook the sliced stem in salted boiling water for 2 minutes. Add the florets and cook for 2 minutes. Drain well, refresh in cold water and drain again.

Purée the coriander or parsley and mint in a food processor. Slowly add the oil, then just before serving, add the vinegar and salt and pepper to taste.

Put the pasta into a serving bowl, pour on a little dressing and toss well. Reserve some of the broccoli, red pepper, pineapple and ham for garnish and add the rest to the pasta.

Pour the remainder of the dressing over the salad and garnish with the reserved salad ingredients.

■ COOK'S TIP

For a salad, pasta must be perfectly cooked. Feed it gradually into a pan of salted fast-boiling water with a spoonful of oil added. Don't cover the pan, and test a strand after 12 minutes for dried, 5 for fresh. Take it out the minute it tastes cooked but still al dente.

169 ANDALUSIAN RICE SALAD

Preparation time:
15 minutes, plus
cooling

Cooking time:
15 minutes

Serves 4

Calories:
412 per portion

YOU WILL NEED:
100 g/4 oz long-grain rice
1 small onion, finely chopped
2 garlic cloves, crushed
1 tablespoon finely chopped fresh
    parsley
6 tablespoons olive oil
1 tablespoon red wine vinegar
1 teaspoon paprika
½ teaspoon salt
½ teaspoon white pepper
450 g/1 lb tomatoes, skinned and
    quartered
4 hard-boiled eggs, quartered
2 red peppers, cored, seeded and
    sliced
2 tablespoons finely chopped fresh
    chervil or 1 teaspoon dried
    chervil

Cook the rice in boiling salted water for 15 minutes or until tender. Drain well and allow to cool.

Put the rice in a mixing bowl and stir in the onion, garlic, parsley, oil, vinegar, paprika, salt and pepper. Pile the mixture in the centre of a large serving dish.

Arrange the tomatoes, eggs and peppers decoratively around the rice and sprinkle with the chopped chervil. Serve at once.

170 NEAPOLITAN SALAD

Preparation time:
10 minutes, plus
chilling

Serves 4

Calories:
348 per portion

YOU WILL NEED:
4 medium tomatoes, skinned and
    quartered
1 small green pepper, cored,
    seeded and thinly sliced
1 small red pepper, cored, seeded
    and thinly sliced
1 small lettuce, shredded
½ x 200 g/7 oz can sweetcorn,
    drained
50 g/2 oz Mozzarella cheese,
    chopped
3 hard-boiled eggs, quartered or
    sliced
3 spring onions, thinly sliced
6 black olives, halved and stoned
120 ml/4 fl oz French dressing
1 garlic clove, finely chopped
½ teaspoon dried oregano
1 tablespoon finely chopped fresh
    basil (optional)

Put the tomatoes, green and red peppers, lettuce, sweetcorn, cheese, egg, spring onions and olives in a large salad bowl. Chill for 20 minutes.

Mix together the French dressing, garlic and oregano in a screw-topped jar and shake vigorously. Pour the dressing over the salad and toss well.

Sprinkle the chopped basil over the top, if using.

■ COOK'S TIP

The chervil - best used fresh - gives a distinctive flavour to this salad. It is a parsley-like herb with feathery leaves.

■ COOK'S TIP

If this salad is to be taken to a picnic, take the dressing in its screw-topped jar and add it a few minutes before serving. This will stop the lettuce going soggy.

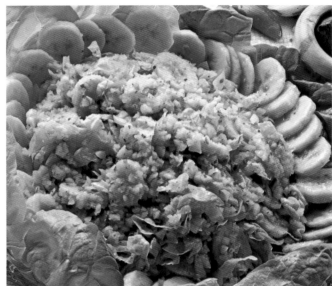

171 THREE BEAN SALAD

Preparation time:
10 minutes, plus
cooling

Cooking time:
5 minutes

Serves 4

Calories:
340 per portion

YOU WILL NEED:
*100 g/4 oz frozen green beans, cut
    into 1 cm/½ inch pieces*
salt
*1 x 439 g/15½ oz can butter
    beans, drained*
*1 x 439 g/15½ oz can red kidney
    beans, drained*
1 onion, chopped
3 tomatoes, quartered
FOR THE DRESSING
4 tablespoons vegetable oil
2 tablespoons white wine vinegar
1 teaspoon French mustard
pinch of sugar
salt and pepper

Cook the green beans in boiling salted water for 5 minutes.
Drain; leave to cool.

Place the green beans, butter beans, kidney beans, onion
and tomatoes in a salad bowl and stir carefully to mix.

Place all the dressing ingredients in a screw-topped jar and
shake until thoroughly mixed. Pour the dressing over the beans
and stir lightly until all the ingredients are coated.

172 BRAZIL NUT SALAD

Preparation time:
5 minutes

Serves 4

Calories:
396 per portion

YOU WILL NEED:
1 crisp lettuce, separated into leaves
*4 tablespoons French dressing
    (see recipe 159)*
3 bananas, peeled and thinly sliced
1 tablespoon lemon juice
*100 g/4 oz Brazil nuts, finely
    chopped*

Arrange half of the lettuce leaves in a shallow salad bowl.
Shred the remaining lettuce into a mixing bowl and pour over
the French dressing. Toss to coat well.

Sprinkle the bananas with the lemon juice. Add half the
bananas and the Brazil nuts to the shredded lettuce and toss to
combine.

Pile the nut and banana mixture on top of the lettuce leaves
in the serving bowl. Arrange the remaining banana slices
around the edge in a ring and serve.

■ COOK'S TIP

*Serve this salad with
barbecued lamb or spare
ribs. For a hotter dressing,
add ½ teaspoon cayenne
pepper to the ingredients.*

■ COOK'S TIP

*If you do not have Brazil
nuts, peanuts (left whole) or
roughly chopped walnuts or
pecans would be suitable
substitutes.*

173 GOI TOM

Preparation time:	YOU WILL NEED:
20 minutes, plus standing	½ cucumber, halved lengthways and seeded
	salt
Serves 6	225 g/8 oz Chinese leaves, finely shredded
	2 carrots, scraped and cut into matchsticks
Calories:	1 small onion, thinly sliced into rings
122 per portion	2 red chillies, seeded and cut into thin strips
	3 pickled gherkins, finely sliced with 3 tablespoons liquid reserved
	1 garlic clove, crushed
	3-4 tablespoons cider vinegar
	50 g/2 oz salted peanuts, lightly crushed
	225 g/8 oz cooked chicken, diced

Cut the cucumber halves into 2.5 cm/1 inch lengths and then into matchsticks. Sprinkle with salt and leave for about 30 minutes.

Put the Chinese leaves into a serving bowl and add the carrots, onion rings, chillies and gherkins, reserving a few onion rings and chilli strips. Drain the cucumber and add to the bowl. Mix the gherkin liquid with the garlic and vinegar and pour over the salad.

Add the nuts and chicken and toss well. Taste and adjust the seasoning and garnish with the remaining onion and chillies and fresh coriander or mint, if liked.

■ COOK'S TIP

Be very careful when handling chillies - do not touch your face or eyes after handling them and be sure to get rid of all the seeds, which are very hot.

174 APRICOT AND TARRAGON SALAD

Preparation time:	YOU WILL NEED:
15 minutes	1 kg/2 lb ripe apricots, peeled
	4 tablespoons soured cream
Serves 4	3 tablespoons tarragon vinegar
	1 tablespoon sugar
Calories:	½ teaspoon salt
98 per portion	large pinch of freshly ground black pepper
	a few fresh tarragon leaves, to garnish

Cut each apricot in half and remove the stones. Arrange the apricots in a glass serving dish. Crack the stones with a nutcracker or hammer and take out the kernels. Chop the kernels and set aside.

To make the dressing, combine the soured cream, vinegar, sugar, salt and pepper. Pour the dressing over the apricots. Sprinkle with the tarragon leaves and chopped kernels and serve.

■ COOK'S TIP

To peel apricots, dip them briefly in boiling water, then plunge them into cold water to loosen the skins. Make a small cut in the skin and peel it off.

175 GRUYERE AND MUSHROOM SALAD

Preparation time:
5 minutes, plus
marinating

Serves 4

Calories:
423 per portion

YOU WILL NEED:
225 g/8 oz Gruyère cheese, cut
   into small cubes
100 g/4 oz button mushrooms,
   quartered
4 large lettuce leaves
1 tablespoon finely chopped fresh
   parsley
FOR THE DRESSING
6 tablespoons olive oil
2 tablespoons red wine vinegar
1 garlic clove, crushed
½ teaspoon salt
large pinch of freshly ground
   black pepper

Put all the dressing ingredients in a screw-topped jar and shake until well mixed. Place the cheese and mushrooms in a mixing bowl and pour over the dressing. Toss to coat and leave for 20 minutes.

Line a shallow salad bowl with the lettuce leaves. Spoon the cheese mixture on top of the lettuce and sprinkle with the chopped parsley. Serve at once.

176 FENNEL SALAD

Preparation time:
5 minutes, plus
chilling

Serves 4

Calories:
128 per portion

YOU WILL NEED:
3 medium heads of fennel, chopped
1 small eating apple, peeled, cored
   and sliced
2 medium tomatoes, skinned and
   diced
2 spring onions, diced
120 ml/4 fl oz French dressing

Put the fennel in a salad bowl. Add the apple, tomatoes and spring onions and stir to mix.

Pour over the French dressing and toss well. Chill in the refrigerator for 1 hour before serving, stirring occasionally.

COOK'S TIP

There should be no need to skin or wash the mushrooms. Just wipe them with absorbent kitchen paper. Trim the stalks neatly.

COOK'S TIP

When trimming the fennel, keep the feathery tops; they will make an attractive garnish for the salad.

177 POTATO AND LEEK SALAD

Preparation time:
10 minutes, plus
chilling

Serves 4

Calories:
342 per portion

YOU WILL NEED:
450 g/1 lb waxy potatoes, cooked,
    peeled and sliced
120 ml/4 fl oz mayonnaise
1 tablespoon lemon juice
1 tablespoon olive oil
½ teaspoon salt
½ teaspoon freshly ground black
    pepper
2 tablespoons finely chopped fresh
    chives
4 tablespoons finely chopped leeks

Place the potatoes in a mixing bowl. Mix together the mayonnaise, lemon juice, oil, salt, pepper and one tablespoon of the chives. Add to the potatoes and toss gently until well coated.

Spoon the mixture into a serving bowl. Sprinkle with the remaining chives and scatter the leeks around the edge of the serving bowl.

Cover and chill for 30 minutes before serving.

178 MIDSUMMER SALAD

Preparation time:
15 minutes, plus
chilling

Serves 4

Calories:
388 per portion

YOU WILL NEED:
250 ml/8 fl oz double cream
1 teaspoon lemon juice
50 g/2 oz button mushrooms,
    thinly sliced
4 small carrots, peeled and grated
large pinch of salt
large pinch of freshly ground
    black pepper
large pinch of grated nutmeg
1 bunch of watercress
½ cucumber, thinly sliced
350 g/12 oz cold cooked meat or
    poultry, thinly sliced
1 small lettuce, shredded

Mix the cream with the lemon juice, and fold in the mushrooms and grated carrots. Season with the salt, pepper and nutmeg. Pile this mixture into the centre of a shallow serving dish and surround it with rings of watercress, cucumber and meat or poultry. Finish with a ring of lettuce. Chill for 20 minutes before serving.

■ COOK'S TIP

The leeks must be well
washed. Trim, cut through
from the top to half way
down and hold under a
running tap to wash out
any dirt between the leaves.

■ COOK'S TIP

The cooked meat in this
salad could be beef, lamb,
pork or ham, or a mixture
of Italian sausages such as
salami or mortadella.

179 RUSSIAN SALAD

Preparation time:
10 minutes, plus
chilling

Serves 4

Calories:
715 per portion

YOU WILL NEED:
*3 large potatoes, cooked, skinned
    and diced*
*4 medium carrots, cooked and
    diced*
*100 g/4 oz French beans, cooked
    and halved*
1 small onion, very finely chopped
100 g/4 oz peas, cooked
50 g/2 oz cooked tongue, diced
100 g/4 oz cooked chicken, diced
50 g/2 oz garlic sausage, diced
250 ml/8 fl oz mayonnaise
large pinch of cayenne pepper
*2 hard-boiled eggs, sliced, to
    garnish*

Put the potatoes, carrots, beans, onions, peas, tongue, chicken
and sausage in a salad bowl. Mix together the mayonnaise and
cayenne and add to the bowl. Toss well. Garnish with the eggs
and chill for about 20 minutes before serving.

180 OX TONGUE AND ORANGE SALAD

Preparation time:
10 minutes

Serves 4

Calories:
179 per portion

YOU WILL NEED:
450 g/1 lb cooked ox tongue, diced
½ teaspoon salt
*large pinch of freshly ground
    black pepper*
4 tablespoons olive oil
4 tablespoons orange juice
*1 tablespoon finely grated lemon
    rind*
4 tablespoons lemon juice
1 tablespoon capers
*6 oranges, peeled, pith removed
    and segmented*
*2 heads of chicory, separated into
    leaves*

Place the ox tongue in a mixing bowl and add the salt, pepper
and one tablespoon of the oil. Mix well.

Add the orange juice, grated lemon rind, lemon juice and
capers to the remaining oil and mix well. Add the orange
segments and orange juice mixture to the ox tongue and stir to
mix.

Line the edge of a shallow serving dish with the chicory
leaves. Pile the ox tongue and orange mixture in the centre.
Serve immediately.

■ COOK'S TIP

*Cooking the potatoes with
their skins on helps keep
the whole potato firm. The
skins come off easily if the
potatoes are still quite
warm when peeled.*

■ COOK'S TIP

*Choose thick-skinned
oranges, as the peel and
pith come off more easily
than with thin-skinned
oranges.*

181 BROAD BEAN AND HAM SALAD

Preparation time:
10 minutes, plus chilling

Cooking time:
5 minutes

Serves 4

Calories:
292 per portion

YOU WILL NEED:
175 g/6 oz thick cut cooked ham, cubed
1 tablespoon Worcestershire sauce
500 g/1 lb broad beans, podded
150 ml/¼ pint soured cream
1 teaspoon chopped fresh chives
large pinch of paprika
½ teaspoon salt
large pinch of freshly ground black pepper
few lettuce leaves
chopped fresh chives, to garnish

Mix the ham with the Worcestershire sauce in a mixing bowl. Leave for 10 minutes.

Meanwhile, cook the beans in boiling salted water for 5 minutes. Drain and refresh under cold running water. Add to the ham with the soured cream, chives, paprika, salt and pepper. Mix well.

Line a shallow salad dish with the lettuce leaves and spoon over the bean and ham mixture. Chill for 30 minutes before serving, garnished with chives.

182 POTATO, BEEF AND TOMATO SALAD

Preparation time:
5 minutes

Serves 4

Calories:
801 per portion

YOU WILL NEED:
1 small lettuce, separated into leaves
1 kg/2 lb cold roast beef, cubed
4 medium potatoes, cooked, peeled and cubed
4 medium tomatoes, skinned, seeded and quartered
4 pickled gherkins, sliced
FOR THE SAUCE
350 ml/12 fl oz soured cream
3 tablespoons horseradish sauce
½ teaspoon salt
½ teaspoon white pepper
2 hard-boiled eggs, thinly sliced, to garnish

Arrange the lettuce leaves on a large, shallow serving plate. Put the meat, potatoes, tomatoes and gherkins in a mixing bowl. Mix together the ingredients for the sauce. Add to the meat mixture and toss gently.

Pile the meat mixture on the lettuce leaves. Garnish with the egg slices and serve at once.

■ COOK'S TIP

For a very quick salad, used canned broad beans, well drained. Canned borlotti or cannellini beans could also be used.

■ COOK'S TIP

To prevent black rings forming round the egg yolks, put the cooked, unshelled eggs under cold running water then leave in cold water until cold.

183 CARDINAL'S SALAD

Preparation time:
25 minutes, plus
soaking

Cooking time:
about 1½ hours

Serves 6

Calories:
186 per portion

YOU WILL NEED:
225 g/8 oz red kidney beans,
  soaked overnight
1.75 litres/3 pints water
6 tablespoons vegetable oil
2 garlic cloves, crushed
4 slices stale bread, cubed, crusts
  removed
1 tablespoon mustard seeds
  (brown or black)
¼ red cabbage, finely shredded
4 spring onions, trimmed and cut
  into fine slivers, to garnish
FOR THE DRESSING
3 tablespoons herb vinegar
6 tablespoons peanut oil
salt and pepper

Drain the beans, rinse and put into a pan with the water. Bring to the boil and boil fast for 10 minutes, lower the heat and simmer for about 1¼ hours until cooked. Drain and rinse well.

In a frying pan, heat the oil gently and fry the garlic until soft. Increase the heat and fry the bread cubes, turning frequently until golden. Drain the croûtons. Fry the mustard seeds in the hot oil for 1 minute until they pop. Remove, drain and reserve.

Toss the cooled beans, cabbage, croûtons and mustard seeds together just before serving.

Mix all the salad dressing ingredients in a screw-topped jar and pour over the salad. Toss well and garnish with the spring onion slivers.

▨ COOK'S TIP

In the absence of mustard seeds use poppy seeds or even caraway, though as caraway is stronger in flavour the quantity must be adjusted to taste.

184 EGYPTIAN SALAD

Preparation time:
15 minutes, plus
soaking

Cooking time:
2 hours 10 minutes

Serves 4
Calories:
301 per portion

YOU WILL NEED:
175 g/6 oz ful medames, soaked
  for 36 hours
salt
fresh coriander leaves
2-3 eggs with white or light-
  coloured shells
brown onion skins
3-4 tablespoons olive oil
1 tablespoon lemon juice
1 garlic clove, crushed
½-1 teaspoon ground cumin
2 tablespoons chopped parsley
fresh coriander, to garnish

Drain the ful medames and cover with fresh water. Bring to the boil, skim, lower the heat and simmer for 2 hours or until tender. Add salt to taste towards the end of the cooking time.

Place a coriander leaf on each egg. Wrap the onion skins around the eggs and then wrap in absorbent kitchen paper to make a parcel. Tie with cotton and cover with cold water. Bring to the boil, cook for 10 minutes and leave to cool. When cold, unwrap and set aside.

Drain and rinse the beans with fresh water, then pop each bean out of its skin, if liked.

Mix the olive oil, lemon juice and garlic, and pour over the beans. Taste and adjust the seasoning.

Transfer the beans to a serving dish and sprinkle with cumin and parsley. Garnish with a sprig of coriander and serve, accompanied by the hard-boiled eggs.

▨ COOK'S TIP

Brown onion skins are traditionally used to colour eggs and to make patterns, as here, with the coriander leaves.

185 WEST AFRICAN BEAN SALAD

Preparation time:
15 minutes, plus
soaking

Cooking time:
45-60 minutes

Serves 4

Calories:
322 per portion

YOU WILL NEED:
225 g/8 oz black-eye beans,
   soaked overnight
4-5 tablespoons peanut oil
1 tablespoon lemon juice or wine
   vinegar
1 garlic clove, crushed
salt and pepper
1 medium onion, red or white,
   sliced
225 g/8 oz large tomatoes, skinned
   and chopped
1 red chilli, cored, seeded and
   chopped (optional)

Drain the beans and cover with fresh water. Bring to the boil, lower the heat and simmer for 45-60 minutes, or until tender. Drain and rinse thoroughly. Transfer to a serving dish.

Blend the oil, lemon juice and garlic and season well with salt and pepper. Pour over the warm beans and leave to cool.

When cool, mix in the onion, tomatoes and chilli, if using.

186 SOYA BEAN SALAD

Preparation time:
10 minutes, plus
soaking

Cooking time:
2-2 1/4 hours

Serves 6-8

Calories:
231 - 173 per portion

YOU WILL NEED:
225 g/8 oz soya beans, soaked
   overnight
4-5 tablespoons olive oil
2 tablespoons lemon juice
1 garlic clove, crushed
salt and pepper
100 g/4 oz bean sprouts, rinsed in
   salted water
½ bunch spring onions, cut into
   shreds

Drain the beans and cover with fresh water. Bring to the boil, lower the heat and simmer for about 2-2¼ hours or until tender. Drain and rinse with cold water. Transfer the drained beans to a serving dish.

Blend the oil, lemon juice and garlic together and pour over the warm beans. Toss well and leave to cool, then season generously with salt and pepper.

Just before serving, mix in most of the bean sprouts and spring onions and garnish with the remainder.

▣ COOK'S TIP

Most pulses are best soaked overnight in fresh cold water. If the atmosphere is very warm soak the beans in the refrigerator to prevent fermentation. Too- *long soaking also causes fermentation.*

▣ COOK'S TIP

Buy the bean sprouts the day they are to be used. They do not keep fresh for long.

187 TUSCAN BEAN SALAD

Preparation time:
10 minutes, plus
soaking

Cooking time:
1 hour

Serves 4-6

Calories:
334 - 222 per portion

YOU WILL NEED:
*225 g/8 oz cannellini or haricot
    beans, soaked overnight*
salt
4 tablespoons olive oil
1 tablespoon lemon juice
*1 x 200 g/7 oz can tuna, drained
    and broken into chunks*
*2 small onions, 1 chopped, 1 sliced
    into rings*
freshly ground black pepper
*chopped basil or parsley, to
    garnish*

Drain the beans and cover with fresh water. Bring to the boil, lower the heat and simmer for about 1 hour. Add salt to taste towards the end of the cooking time. Drain and rinse.

Blend the oil and lemon juice and pour over the warm beans. Toss with the tuna and the chopped onion. Taste and adjust the seasoning.

Turn into a serving dish and garnish with the onion rings and chopped basil or parsley.

188 TABBOULEH

Preparation time:
20 minutes, plus
soaking and chilling

Serves 4

Calories:
432 per portion

YOU WILL NEED:
175 g/6 oz bulgur (cracked wheat)
*½ cucumber, halved, seeded and
    coarsely grated*
salt
50 g/2 oz finely chopped parsley
4 tablespoons finely chopped mint
*3 firm tomatoes, skinned, seeded
    and diced*
*½ bunch spring onions, finely
    shredded*
8 tablespoons grapeseed oil
3 tablespoons lemon juice
freshly ground black pepper
½ crisp lettuce

Soak the bulgur in cold water to cover for about 30 minutes.

Sprinkle the cucumber with salt. Set aside for 15 minutes then rinse and drain.

Drain the bulgur through a fine strainer and squeeze as dry as possible.

Stir the cucumber, parsley, mint and tomatoes into the bulgur with some of the spring onions.

Pour over the oil and lemon juice. Season with salt and pepper and mix lightly. Cover with cling film and chill for an hour or so.

Serve in a bowl lined with lettuce leaves and garnish with the remaining spring onions.

▨ COOK'S TIP

When overnight soaking is not possible: cover beans with cold water, bring to the boil and cook rapidly for 2 minutes. Remove from the heat, cover and leave on one side for 1 hour. Remove the lid and cook in the same water until tender, remembering to fast boil kidney beans for the first 10 minutes.

▨ COOK'S TIP

Bulgur is also known as burghul or cracked wheat. It should not be confused with knibbled or crushed wheat which is not suitable for the same purposes.

189 SPICED RICE SALAD

Preparation time: 10 minutes	YOU WILL NEED: 225 g/8 oz basmati or long-grain rice, washed
Cooking time: 20 minutes	600 ml/1 pint water salt ½-1 teaspoon powdered turmeric
Serves 4	1 teaspoon coriander seeds ½ teaspoon cumin seeds

Calories:
452 per portion
	6 tablespoons peanut oil
	3-4 tablespoons lemon juice
	2-3 hard-boiled eggs, whites and
	    yolks separated
	2 red chillies, cored, seeded and
	    shredded
	fresh coriander leaves, to garnish

Put the rice into a pan with the water, salt and turmeric. Bring to the boil. Lower the heat, cover and cook gently for 10-15 minutes or until all the water is absorbed and the rice is tender.

Meanwhile dry-fry the coriander seeds for 1-2 minutes in a pan over gentle heat. Remove from the heat, cool and crush the seeds. Set aside and repeat with the cumin seeds.

Turn the rice into a bowl, pour over the peanut oil and lemon juice. Fork through, adding the crushed coriander and cumin. Leave to cool.

Chop the egg whites and sieve the yolks. Reserve 1 tablespoon egg yolk for the garnish. Just before serving, mix the rice with the egg whites, yolks and half the chilli.

Pile into serving bowls and garnish with the reserved egg yolk, chilli and the coriander leaves.

■ COOK'S TIP

For a more delicate flavour, use saffron instead of turmeric. Soak the strands in 3 tablespoons hot water for 5 minutes, then strain the liquid into the rice.

190 LICHFIELD'S WARM SALAD

Preparation time: 20 minutes	YOU WILL NEED: 150 ml/¼ pint medium dry Madeira

Cooking time:
10 minutes
	300 ml/½ pint chicken stock
	salad leaves from radicchio,
	    Webb's or iceberg lettuce,
	    chicory, mache and watercress,
	    torn into small pieces

Serves 4	6-8 tablespoons French dressing (see recipe 159)

Calories:
386 per portion
	50 g/2 oz butter, cut into small
	    pieces
	4 chicken livers, trimmed and
	    quartered
	2 duck livers, trimmed and
	    quartered
	salt and pepper
	12 grapes, skinned (optional),
	    halved and seeded
	a little chopped parsley, to garnish

Fast boil the Madeira wine to reduce it by half, add the stock and fast boil again to reduce it by half. Reserve.

Put the salad leaves into a bowl and pour over the French dressing. Divide between four plates.

Melt 25 g/1 oz butter in a frying pan and gently fry the chicken and duck livers for 30 seconds on each side. Season with salt and pepper and arrange on top of the salads.

Bring the wine mixture to the boil. Add the remaining butter and stir in the grapes. Spoon over the salad, sprinkle with parsley and serve.

■ COOK'S TIP

Chicken livers are readily available. Duck livers may be more hard to find. Ask a butcher who sells duck portions. The livers should only be cooked for a short time so that they are still pink inside.

191 POTATO SALAD

Preparation time:
10 minutes

Cooking time:
15-20 minutes

Serves 4

Calories:
131 per portion

YOU WILL NEED:
450 g/1 lb new potatoes, washed
2 teaspoons olive oil
1 teaspoon white wine vinegar
4 tablespoons soured cream
salt and pepper
1 tablespoon snipped chives, to
   garnish

Cook the potatoes in boiling salted water for 15-20 minute, or until just tender. Drain, and when cool enough to handle cut into 1 cm/½ inch pieces. Place in a salad bowl.

Combine the oil and vinegar and pour over the potatoes while still warm, so that they absorb the dressing. Leave to cool.

Whisk the soured cream with a fork, then using a wooden spoon, carefully mix it into the potatoes without breaking them up. Season with salt and pepper. Sprinkle with the chives before serving.

192 SALADE COMTESSE

Preparation time:
10 minutes

Cooking time:
15 minutes

Serves 4-6

Calories:
450 - 300 per
portion

YOU WILL NEED:
225 g/8 oz long-grain rice
600 ml/1 pint water
salt
6 tablespoons corn oil
3 tablespoons herb vinegar
1 x 200 g/7 oz can tuna fish in oil
100 g/4 oz button mushrooms,
   wiped and sliced
1 small onion, chopped
2 pickled gherkins, diced
freshly ground black pepper
3 tablespoons mixed chopped
   parsley and chives

Put the rice into a pan with the water and salt. Bring to the boil, then cover and simmer over a low heat for 12-15 minutes until all the water has been absorbed and the rice grains are tender.

Pour over the corn oil and vinegar and fork through. Turn into a bowl and leave to cool.

Break the tuna fish into bite-size pieces with its oil and add to the rice with the mushrooms, onion, gherkins and pepper to taste. Stir in 2 tablespoons of the parsley and chives.

Serve garnished with the remaining herbs.

COOK'S TIP

Serve this salad with hamburgers and barbecued chops and steaks. For a variation, add 4 finely chopped spring onions to the salad with the cream.

COOK'S TIP

The rice can be prepared and dressed with the oil and vinegar dressing several hours ahead. Leave, covered, in a cool place.

SAUCES, DIPS & MARINADES

The marinades and sauces included in this chapter can be used to tenderize meat and poultry before barbecuing or grilling and to add flavour during the cooking process. There are also dressings to give extra zest and interest to even the simplest salad.

193 RED WINE MARINADE

Preparation time:
5 minutes

Makes about
300 ml/1/2 pint

Total calories: 482

YOU WILL NEED:
150 ml/¼ pint red wine
2 tablespoons lemon juice
1 onion, sliced
1 carrot, sliced
1 celery stalk, chopped
1 parsley sprig or ½ teaspoon
    dried parsley
1 thyme sprig or ½ teaspoon
    dried thyme
1 bay leaf
6 black peppercorns, lightly
    crushed
3 tablespoons vegetable oil
    (optional; see method)

Combine all the ingredients in a large bowl and leave to stand for about 1 hour before adding the food to be marinated. Add the oil only if the marinade is to be used for lean meat such as chicken, turkey or venison.

Marinate poultry for 2-4 hours, beef or lamb for kebabs for 1-2 hours, and large joints for up to 12 hours in the refrigerator. Turn the food several times during marinating.

Use the excess marinade to baste the food during cooking.

194 YOGURT MARINADE

Preparation time:
5 minutes

Makes about
500 ml/18 fl oz

Total calories: 610

YOU WILL NEED:
450 ml/¾ pint natural yogurt
3 tablespoons olive oil
2 tablespoons fresh lime juice
1 small onion, grated
1 teaspoon ground cloves
1 teaspoon cumin seeds, crushed
¼ teaspoon ground cardamom
2 garlic cloves, crushed
1 teaspoon ground cinnamon
1 teaspoon salt
1 teaspoon freshly ground white
    pepper

Mix all the ingredients together thoroughly in a large bowl, then chill up to 24 hours and use as required.

■ COOK'S TIP

White wine may be substituted for red to marinate veal, pork, poultry or fish. Add some minced garlic to the marinade for extra flavour.

■ COOK'S TIP

This marinade not only makes meat and poultry of all kind succulent and tender, it is also delicious with white fish and makes an aromatic dipping sauce *to serve with sticks of raw vegetables or pitta bread.*

195 GUINNESS MARINADE

Preparation time:
6 minutes

Makes about
300 ml/½ pint

Total calories: 168

YOU WILL NEED:
2 teaspoons Dijon mustard
5 cloves
1 ½ tablespoons soft dark brown
  sugar
1 x 5cm/2 inch piece cinnamon
  stick, crumbled
6 whole black peppercorns, lightly
  crushed
300 ml/½ pint Guinness

Mix the mustard with all the ingredients except the Guinness, then gradually pour on the Guinness, stirring constantly.

Leave for 3-4 minutes to let the sugar dissolve, then stir again and use as required.

196 TENDERIZING MARINADE

Preparation time:
5 minutes, plus
standing

Makes about
300 ml/½ pint

Total calories: 36

YOU WILL NEED:
150 ml/¼ pint malt or wine
  vinegar
150 ml/¼ pint water
1 large onion, sliced
6 cloves
2 bay leaves
6 black peppercorns, slightly
  crushed
1 teaspoon salt

Mix all the ingredients together and leave for at least 12 hours before using. Use for tenderizing tougher cuts of meat such as rib joints, top rump, breast of lamb and spare ribs, by allowing them to stand in the mixture for 24-36 hours in the refrigerator. For smaller cuts such as steaks, chops and skewered food, 1-5 hours marinating is sufficient.

███ COOK'S TIP

This rich, sweet marinade does not have to be confined to barbecue cooking. It's delicious with roast beef, and makes steak and kidney pie taste great.

███ COOK'S TIP

As barbecued meat is cooked quickly, it needs to be tender to cook successfully. It is the acid in the marinade - wine, vinegar or lemon juice - *which helps to tenderize the meat.*

197 SOURED CREAM MARINADE

Preparation time:	YOU WILL NEED:
5 minutes	*1 x 150 ml/5 fl oz carton soured*
	cream
Makes about	*1 tablespoon lemon juice*
150 ml/1/4 pint	*1 garlic clove, crushed*
	salt and pepper
Total calories: 165	*1 celery stalk, thinly sliced*
	large pinch of paprika
	½ teaspoon Worcestershire sauce

Put the soured cream in a bowl and add the lemon juice, garlic and salt and pepper to taste. Mix well. Stir in the celery, paprika and Worcestershire sauce.

198 BARBECUE SAUCE

Preparation time:	YOU WILL NEED:
10 minutes	*50 g/2 oz margarine or butter*
	1 large onion, chopped
Cooking time:	*2 teaspoons tomato purée*
16 minutes	*2 tablespoons wine vinegar*
	1 tablespoon lemon juice
Serves 4-6	*2 tablespoons demerara sugar*
	2 teaspoons English mustard
Calories:	*2 tablespoons Worcestershire sauce*
157 - 105 per portion	*1 teaspoon clear honey*
	pinch of mixed dried herbs
	1 teaspoon chilli seasoning
	150 ml/¼ pint water
	salt and pepper

Melt the margarine in a saucepan, add the onion and fry gently for 5 minutes until soft. Raise the heat a little, add all the other ingredients and stir well.

Bring the sauce to the boil, then reduce the heat and simmer for about 10 minutes until well combined and syrupy. Serve immediately.

■ COOK'S TIP

Use this marinade for steak, lamb chops, chicken portions and skewered food, allowing 2-4 hours depending on the size of the meat.

■ COOK'S TIP

Make this sauce in advance then reheat it in a pan over the barbecue. Serve with chicken, hamburgers and spare ribs. Use chicken stock instead of water.

199 MEXICAN CHILLI SAUCE

Preparation time:	YOU WILL NEED:
10 minutes	2 tablespoons vegetable oil
	1 large onion, finely chopped
Cooking time:	1 green pepper, cored, seeded and
about 30 minutes	finely chopped
	1 x 397 g/14 oz can tomatoes
Serves 4-6	1 x 198 g/7 oz can red pimientos,
	drained and chopped
Calories:	1 teaspoon sugar
107 - 71 per portion	large pinch of English mustard
	powder
	pinch of chilli powder
	1 tablespoon lemon juice
	salt and pepper
	1 tablespoon chopped fresh parsley

Heat the oil in a saucepan and add the onion and green pepper. Fry gently for 5 minutes until the onion is soft and lightly coloured.

Add the tomatoes with their juice, breaking them down with a wooden spoon, the pimientos, sugar, mustard powder, chilli powder, lemon juice and salt and pepper to taste. Stir well and bring to the boil.

Simmer gently for 20 minutes until the vegetables are tender and the ingredients are well combined.

Stir in the parsley just before serving.

200 CORN RELISH

Preparation time:	YOU WILL NEED:
10 minutes	600 ml/1 pint white wine vinegar
	75 g/3 oz sugar
Cooking time:	1 tablespoon mustard seeds or 1
about 25 minutes	teaspoon English mustard
	powder
Makes about	1 teaspoon salt
1 kg/2 lb	450 g/1 lb sweetcorn kernels, fresh
	or frozen
Total calories: 888	1 green pepper, cored, seeded and
	finely chopped
	1 red pepper, cored, seeded and
	finely chopped
	1 onion, finely chopped
	4 celery stalks, finely sliced

In a large bowl, mix a little of the vinegar with the sugar, mustard and salt to make a smooth paste, then stir in the remaining vinegar.

Pour the mixture into a large saucepan and bring slowly to the boil. Add the vegetables to the pan and simmer, uncovered, for 20 minutes or until the vegetables are just tender.

Pour into clean, warm jars or bottles and seal with a vinegar-proof cover. Label and store.

■ COOK'S TIP

This piquant sauce goes well with fish or chicken pieces. For a milder sauce, omit the chilli powder and add 1 teaspoon Worcestershire sauce.

■ COOK'S TIP

For a hotter flavour, use 1 red chilli, seeded and chopped, instead of the red pepper. For a different taste substitute cider vinegar for the white wine vinegar.

201 PEPPER RELISH

Preparation time:	YOU WILL NEED:
20 minutes	*4 firm tomatoes*
	1 onion
Cooking time:	*1 green pepper*
about 1 hour	*2 fresh green chillies*
	2 stalks celery
Makes 4-6 portions	*1 teaspoon salt*
	½ teaspoon ginger
Calories:	*½ teaspoon cinnamon*
60 - 40 per portion	*pinch of ground cloves*
	4 tablespoons pickling vinegar
	4 tablespoons brown sugar

Peel, seed and chop the tomatoes. Peel and chop the onion. Dice the pepper and chillies, discarding the core seeds and white pith. (Take care not to touch the face or eyes after chopping the chillies.) Finely chop the celery. Place the prepared vegetables with all the remaining ingredients in a medium saucepan and bring to the boil. Lower the heat and simmer gently for 1 hour. Serve hot or cold.

Store in an airtight container in the refrigerator for up to 2 weeks. Serve with barbecued and cold meats.

202 SWEETCORN AND CUCUMBER RELISH

Preparation time:	YOU WILL NEED:
10 minutes, plus chilling	*2 sticks celery*
	½ cucumber
	1 x 200 g/7 oz can sweetcorn niblets
Serves 4	*4 tablespoons cider vinegar*
	2 tablespoons vegetable oil
Calories:	*1 tablespoon sugar*
124 per portion	*½ teaspoon salt*
	½ teaspoon celery, cumin, or
	coriander seeds

Dice the celery and cucumber finely; drain the sweetcorn and mix with the remaining ingredients. Place in a serving bowl and refrigerate for 2 hours before serving. Serve with hot or cold meats and salads. Store in the fridge for up to 3 days.

■ COOK'S TIP

As this relish is cooked, it can be kept for a time; if you want to keep it for a long period of time, bottle it while hot in sterilised screw-topped jars and keep in the refrigerator for up to 3 months.

■ COOK'S TIP

Sweet and crunchy, this relish should be made at least 2 hours before serving.

203 PIQUANT TOMATO RELISH

Preparation time:	YOU WILL NEED:
15 minutes	*1 kg/2 lb tomatoes*
	½ cucumber
Makes 8-10 portions	*4 sticks celery*
	6-8 small gherkins
Calories:	FOR THE DRESSING
86 - 69 per portion	*4 tablespoons vegetable oil*
	2 tablespoons malt vinegar
	1 teaspoon salt
	½ teaspoon dry mustard
	½ teaspoon caster sugar
	a few shakes of Tabasco sauce (optional)

Place the tomatoes in a bowl and cover with boiling water. Leave for 1 minute; drain, then peel. Roughly chop the tomatoes; place in a medium-sized bowl. Dice the cucumber into 5-mm/¼-inch cubes. Wash and slice the celery, slice the gherkins. Add to the chopped tomatoes. Mix the dressing ingredients together, add to the tomato mixture and stir until well coated. Cover and leave in a cool place for 1 hour. The relish can be kept in a plastic container in the refrigerator for up to 1 week.

204 MINT CHUTNEY

Preparation time:	YOU WILL NEED:
10 minutes	*2 spring onions, chopped*
	2 tablespoons chopped fresh mint
Serves 4	*½ teaspoon salt*
	1 teaspoon sugar
Calories:	*1 small green chilli, seeded and*
14 per portion	*chopped, or large pinch of chilli powder*
	large pinch of garam masala
	1 tablespoon lemon juice
	2 tablespoons natural yoghurt

Place all the ingredients in a blender and reduce to a purée. Taste the mixture and add more salt and sugar, if necessary.

■ COOK'S TIP

This crisp, fresh relish sharpens burgers, sausages, and most barbecued meats.

■ COOK'S TIP

This Indian-style chutney is best served fresh but it may be kept for up to 2 days in the refrigerator, if you wish.

205 PEANUT SAUCE

Preparation time:
30 minutes, plus
marinating

Cooking time:
20 minutes

Serves 4-6

Calories:
475 - 316 per portion

YOU WILL NEED:
225 g/8 oz dry roast peanuts, or
    salted peanuts, well rinsed and
    drained
2 large garlic cloves, halved
3 dried red chillies, seeded and
    crushed
1 medium onion, coarsely
    chopped
1 teaspoon salt
4 tablespoons peanut oil
100 ml/3½ fl oz chicken stock
1 tablespoon soft dark brown sugar
2 tablespoons soy sauce
2 tablespoons lime juice

Put the peanuts into a grinder and grind finely, then transfer to
a blender. Add the garlic, chillies, onion, salt and half the
peanut oil and liquidize to a thick purée, adding 1 tablespoon
of the chicken stock if necessary to make it blend easily.

Heat the remaining oil in a small saucepan, pour in the
purée and gently cook for 3-4 minutes, stirring constantly.

Add the chicken stock, bring to the boil, then lower the
heat and gently simmer for 5-10 minutes until it is very thick
and smooth.

Remove from the heat and stir in the sugar, soy sauce and
lime juice, mixing well.

206 SWEET AND SOUR SAUCE

Preparation time:
8 minutes

Cooking time:
15 minutes

Makes about
300 ml/1/2 pint

Total calories: 288

YOU WILL NEED:
1 x 400 g/14 oz can tomatoes
2 green peppers, cored, seeded and
    diced
2 tablespoons cornflour
4 tablespoons vinegar
2 tablespoons sugar
150 ml/¼ pint tomato juice
1 tablespoon soy sauce
salt and pepper

Put the tomatoes with the can juice in a saucepan and break
them down with a wooden spoon. Stir in the green peppers.
Bring to the boil and simmer for 5 minutes. Dissolve the
cornflour in the vinegar and add to the tomato mixture with
the remaining ingredients and salt and pepper to taste. Stir well
and cook for 10 minutes.

■ COOK'S TIP

A delicacy of Indonesia, this
is the sauce usually served
with satay chicken or pork.
It may be made up 24 hours
in advance.

■ COOK'S TIP

This sauce is ideal for
serving with pork. To vary
the flavour, dice 2 slices of
canned pineapple and cook
for 10 minutes with the
other ingredients.

207 COCONUT MINT SAUCE

Preparation time:
10 minutes, plus
soaking and chilling

Makes about
175 ml/6 fl oz

Total calories: 442

YOU WILL NEED:
50 g/2 oz desiccated coconut
150 ml/5 fl oz natural yogurt
grated rind of 1 lime
3 tablespoons lime juice
1 x 2.5 cm/1 inch piece fresh root
  ginger, peeled and grated
8 tablespoons finely chopped and
  lightly pounded fresh mint
1 clove garlic, crushed
salt

Put the coconut into a bowl, pour over the yogurt and stir. Cover, then leave for 1 hour.

Put the soaked coconut and yogurt into a blender and liquidize to a thick purée.

Add the remaining ingredients, blend again for 1 minute, then pour the sauce into a bowl. Chill for at least 30 minutes before serving.

208 CURRY SPICE SAUCE

Preparation time:
20 minutes

Cooking time:
about 1 hour 10
minutes

Serves 4

Calories:
123 per portion

YOU WILL NEED:
4 cloves
2 teaspoons coriander seeds
1 teaspoon cumin seeds
½ teaspoon ginger
1 teaspoon turmeric
¼ teaspoon cinnamon
¼ teaspoon chilli powder
2 tablespoons oil
225 g/8 oz onions, sliced
2 garlic cloves, crushed
2 tablespoons plain flour
6 tomatoes, peeled, seeded and
  chopped
300 ml/½ pint hot chicken stock
1 teaspoon granulated sugar
salt

Place the cloves and coriander seeds in a basin; crush with the end of a rolling pin. Chop cumin seeds; add to the basin with the ginger, turmeric, cinnamon and chilli powder. Alternatively, blend in a liquidiser.

Heat the oil in a saucepan and fry the spices for 2 minutes. Add the onions and garlic; cook until soft - about 5 minutes. Stir in the flour and tomatoes; cook for 2 minutes, then add the stock. Bring to the boil; cover and simmer for 1 hour or until the tomatoes are broken down and the sauce is thick. Add sugar; taste and add salt, if necessary.

■ COOK'S TIP

This is a wonderfully cooling dip, ideal for serving with hot spicy kebabs. It will keep for up to a day in the refrigerator if made in advance.

■ COOK'S TIP

Serve this potent sauce with barbecued sausages, chops or chicken.

209 COCONUT SATAY SAUCE

Preparation time:
15 minutes, plus
standing

Cooking time:
15-20 minutes

Serves 4

Calories:
175 per portion

YOU WILL NEED:
1 small onion, finely chopped
1 garlic clove, crushed
salt
4 tablespoons desiccated coconut
1 tablespoon oil
juice of ½ lemon
4 level tablespoons peanut butter
½ level teaspoon chilli powder
1 level teaspoon soft brown sugar
1 bay leaf

Place the coconut in a jug and add 300 ml/½ pint boiling water. Leave for 15 minutes, then strain in a sieve, reserving the liquid, pressing until all the liquid is removed from the coconut.

Heat the oil in a saucepan. Add the onion and garlic, and fry until the onion is tender. Stir in the coconut liquid, lemon juice, peanut butter, chilli powder, sugar and bay leaf. Bring to the boil, stirring; cover and simmer for 10-15 minutes, until the sauce has thickened. Taste and add more salt if necessary. Remove the bay leaf and serve the sauce hot.

210 FINES HERBES VINAIGRETTE

Preparation time:
15 minutes

Makes
250 ml/8 fl oz

Total calories: 1551

YOU WILL NEED:
½ teaspoon finely chopped fresh
    chervil
1 teaspoon finely chopped fresh
    chives
1 tablespoon finely chopped parsley
1 teaspoon prepared French
    mustard
½ teaspoon salt
large pinch of freshly ground
    black pepper
1 garlic clove, crushed
175 ml/6 fl oz olive oil
4 tablespoons tarragon vinegar
2 teaspoons lemon juice

Put all the ingredients in a screw-topped jar and shake vigorously until well mixed. Use as required, storing in the refrigerator.

■ COOK'S TIP

This is delicious spread over pork or chicken during the last few minutes of barbecuing, or served as an accompaniment to plain grilled food.

■ COOK'S TIP

Do not be tempted to use dried herbs in this delicious salad dressing. The tang of fresh herbs is essential to a good herb vinaigrette.

211 EGG AND CAPER DRESSING

Preparation time:
10 minutes

Makes
100 ml/3 1/2 fl oz

Total calories: 512

YOU WILL NEED:
3 hard-boiled egg yolks
2 teaspoons prepared French
  mustard
1 small garlic clove, crushed
½ teaspoon salt
large pinch of freshly ground
  black pepper
pinch of dill seed
2 tablespoons olive oil
1½ teaspoons white wine
  vinegar
2 tablespoons lemon juice
1½ teaspoons finely chopped
  capers

Rub the egg yolks through a fine sieve into a small mixing bowl. Add the mustard, garlic, salt, pepper and dill and beat briskly until the mixture forms a smooth paste. Stir in the oil, a little at a time, then add the vinegar and lemon juice. Mix well and stir in the capers.

Chill for 30 minutes and serve as required.

212 THOUSAND ISLAND DRESSING

Preparation time:
15 minutes, plus chilling

Makes
600 ml/1 pint

Total calories: 3657

YOU WILL NEED:
450 ml/¾ pint mayonnaise
1 teaspoon Tabasco sauce
2 tablespoons finely chopped
pimientos or sweet pickle
10 stuffed green olives, finely
  chopped
2 hard-boiled eggs, very finely
  chopped
1 medium shallot, very finely
  chopped
3 tablespoons olive oil
½ teaspoon salt
½ teaspoon pepper
1 tablespoon wine vinegar

Mix together all the ingredients. Pour into a serving bowl and chill for at least 1 hour before serving.

■ COOK'S TIP

Use this dressing to add interest to a simple salad of crisp, green leaves.

■ COOK'S TIP

This dressing gives piquancy to all kinds of salad. Use it, too, in sandwiches and with cold meats like ham and salami.

SWEETS

Summertime desserts and sweets are best kept deliciously light, using lots of the fresh fruits of all kinds that are so abundant in summer and autumn. Sweet foods for putting in picnic hampers and cool boxes also need to be easily packed and carried. There are recipes in this chapter which fulfill all these requirements, offering a good variety of desserts, biscuits and cakes.

213 BARBECUED MARSHMALLOWS

Preparation time:
5 minutes

Cooking time:
2-4 minutes

**Makes about 24
cubes**

Calories:
96 per portion

YOU WILL NEED:
*1 x 120 g/4½ oz packet of
    marshmallows*

Thread the marshmallows on to skewers, allowing one skewer per person. Thread 4-6 marshmallows on each skewer.

Cook the marshmallows carefully over hot coals for 2-4 minutes until they are browned on the outside: inside they will be melted and hot.

Leave the marshmallows for a minute or so before taking them off the skewers and eating them; don't let them get cold.

214 CHOCOLATE GONE BANANAS

Preparation time:
5 minutes

Cooking time:
about 10 minutes

Serves 4

Calories:
320 per portion

YOU WILL NEED:
*4 ripe bananas
about 175 g/6 oz plain chocolate*

Make a small slit in each banana skin and insert one or two squares of chocolate. Wrap each banana in foil and cook amongst the hot coals for about 10 minutes.

Don't be put off by the blackened skins; the fruit is delicious when split open.

■ COOK'S TIP

Another way of serving marshmallows which is popular with children is to melt them in a heatproof bowl until they are completely runny and then *to give each child a peeled, fresh banana which they can then dip into the marshmallow fondue.*

■ COOK'S TIP

As an alternative to plain chocolate, use squares of dark chocolate with roasted almonds or, for adults, liqueur-filled chocolate squares.

SWEETS

215 BARBADOS BAKED PINEAPPLE

Preparation time:
10 minutes

Cooking time:
10-15 minutes

Serves 4

Calories:
261 per portion

YOU WILL NEED:
1 ripe pineapple
75 g/3 oz soft brown sugar
½ teaspoon ground ginger
50 g/2 oz desiccated coconut
strawberries, to decorate

Cut a fresh pineapple into thick rings. Place each ring on a separate square of foil and sprinkle with a little brown sugar and pinch of ginger. Top with desiccated coconut. Wrap the foil securely around the slices and seal.

Cook over warm coals for 10-15 minutes. Serve on individual plates, decorated with strawberries.

216 CELESTIAL PINEAPPLE

Preparation time:
20 minutes, plus standing

Serves 6-8

Calories:
110 - 83 per portion

YOU WILL NEED:
1 ripe pineapple
300 g/11 oz canned lychees
½ small watermelon
2 tablespoons dark rum

Cut the pineapple in half lengthways, scoop out the flesh and cut into bite-sized pieces, discarding any woody core. Drain the lychees and reserve the syrup. Remove the seeds from the watermelon and scoop out the flesh with a melon-baller or small spoon.

Mix together the syrup from the lychees and the dark rum.

Place the pineapple pieces, melon balls and lychees in a bowl and pour the rum syrup over. Leave to stand for about 20 minutes. Spoon the mixed fruit into the pineapple halves and serve.

■ COOK'S TIP

Freshly grated coconut makes this dessert something special. Bore a hole through two of the eyes of a coconut and drain off the liquid. The coconut will crack more easily if put in the oven at 150 C/300 F/gas 2 for 20 minutes, then tap lightly with a hammer, if necessary.

■ COOK'S TIP

On a very hot day, the pineapple halves can be arranged on a tray and surrounded by crushed ice. Fig leaves also make an effective tray lining.

217 BAKED PINEAPPLE SLICES

Preparation time:
5 minutes, plus
standing

Cooking time:
about 20 minutes

Serves 4

Calories:
101 per portion

YOU WILL NEED:
4 thick slices fresh pineapple,
   peeled and cored
4 tablespoons soft light brown
   sugar
2 tablespoons kirsch
mint sprigs, to decorate

Place each pineapple slice in the centre of a square of foil large enough to contain it. Sprinkle 1 tablespoon sugar over each slice, then sprinkle the kirsch over the top. Leave to stand for about 30 minutes and then seal the foil edges firmly to make parcels.

Cook the pineapple parcels over hot coals for about 20 minutes, turning once, until the pineapple is tender.

Open the parcels and decorate with mint sprigs. Serve with whipped cream or scoops of ice cream.

218 BRANDIED CREAM CHEESE AND RASPBERRIES

Preparation time:
15 minutes, plus
soaking and chilling

Serves 6-8

Calories:
479 - 359 per portion

YOU WILL NEED:
100 g/4 oz sultanas
150 ml/¼ pint brandy
400 g/14 oz mascarpone cheese
75 g/3 oz icing sugar
125 ml/4 fl oz double cream,
   lightly whipped
225 g/8 oz raspberries

Place the sultanas in a bowl, cover with brandy and leave to soak for 30 minutes.

Mix the mascarpone, sugar and lightly whipped cream together, then add the sultanas and brandy, stirring thoroughly so that the brandy is completely absorbed.

Place the mixture in a shallow dish and make a slight indentation with the back of a spoon in the centre of the cheese. Chill for 1 hour.

Just before serving, pile the raspberries into the indentation in the middle of the cheese and serve immediately, accompanied by langue de chats biscuits or sponge fingers, if liked.

■ COOK'S TIP

Halved grapefruit may be baked in the same way, using 2 tablespoons of gin instead of the kirsch if liked. Omit the cream or ice cream.

■ COOK'S TIP

Mascarpone is a full-fat double cream cheese from Italy. Most supermarkets now stock it, but, if you can't find it, an acceptable substitute would be to mix a good cream cheese with double cream in the ratio of 2:1.

219 LYCHEE AND REDCURRANT SORBETS

Preparation time:
30 minutes, plus freezing

Cooking time:
20 minutes

Serves 6-8

Calories:
122 - 92 per portion

YOU WILL NEED:
375 g/13 oz canned lychees, with 6 tablespoons of the juice reserved
2 tablespoons lemon juice
1 tablespoon Kirsch
1 egg white
FOR THE REDCURRANT SORBET
400 g/14 oz redcurrants, stalks removed
75 g/3 oz caster sugar
3 tablespoons rosewater
1 egg white
caster sugar to serve

Blend the lychees with the reserved juice, lemon juice and Kirsch to a purée. Pour the mixture into a freezer-proof container and freeze for 3 hours.

Place the redcurrants in a saucepan with the sugar, add 6 tablespoons water and simmer gently for 20 minutes, stirring once or twice, until the currants are very soft. Blend the redcurrants to a purée and then rub them through a sieve to remove the seeds. Stir in the rosewater, then place in another freezer-proof container and freeze for 3 hours.

Take the lychees out of the freezer and beat with a fork until slushy. Whisk the egg white until soft peaks form, fold into the lychees and return the mixture to the freezer. Do the same with the frozen redcurrant purée. After 1 hour, whisk up both mixtures again and then return them to the freezer for a further 2 hours before serving.

■ COOK'S TIP

This sorbet may be kept frozen for up to 2 months, but take it out of the freezer and whisk up 2 hours before serving, then return to the freezer. To frost the rims of the serving glasses, wet the rims with cold water then dip into caster sugar.

220 PEACH PACKETS

Preparation time:
10 minutes

Cooking time:
20-30 minutes

Serves 6

Calories:
338 per portion

YOU WILL NEED:
6 large peaches, peeled, cut in half and stoned
75 g/3 oz butter
6 tablespoons dry vermouth
6 teaspoons orange-flower water
6 tablespoons soft brown cane sugar

Cut out six large pieces of heavy-duty foil and grease each one lightly. If heavy-duty foil is not available, use a double layer of ordinary kitchen foil.

Place two peach halves on each square of foil and dot each peach with small pieces of butter. Pour 1 tablespoon vermouth over each peach and then 1 teaspoon of the orange-flower water. Sprinkle 1 tablespoon sugar over each peach and carefully fold over the edges of the foil to make a leakproof parcel. Wrap all the parcels in a very large piece of foil to avoid tearing.

Cook the parcels over hot coals for 20-30 minutes. If the coals are very hot the peaches will need the lesser time. Unwrap the parcels carefully and transfer the peaches to a platter. Serve the peaches with the juices from the parcels poured over, accompanied by chilled double cream.

■ COOK'S TIP

If the peaches are slightly hard, cut a cross in the stalk end of each one and blanch them in boiling water for 2 minutes; the skins will then peel off easily.

221 BAKED BANANAS

Preparation time:
5 minutes

Cooking time:
10-15 minutes

Serves 6

Calories:
264 per portion

YOU WILL NEED:
6 large ripe bananas, unpeeled
FOR THE CHANTILLY CREAM
175 ml/6 fl oz whipping cream
2 tablespoons strong coffee
50 g/2 oz icing sugar
2 tablespoons dark rum

Wipe the bananas and set them aside.

Whip the cream until soft peaks form; add the coffee and beat again. Fold in the icing sugar and then the rum. Place the mixture in a small bowl and chill until required.

Arrange the unpeeled bananas on a greased grid over hot coals and cook for 10-15 minutes until they are blackened on the outside and feel very soft.

Put the bananas on serving plates, make a 2.5 cm/1 inch slit in each one and let people peel them and dip them into the Chantilly cream.

222 CARAMELIZED PINEAPPLE

Preparation time:
10 minutes, plus marinating

Cooking time:
10 minutes

Serves 6-8

Calories:
180 - 135 per portion

YOU WILL NEED:
1 large ripe pineapple, cut into
   slices about 2 cm/¼ inch thick
175 g/6 oz dark brown cane sugar
4 tablespoons white rum

Lay the pineapple slices on a plate or tray. Mix together the brown sugar and the rum, then brush the mixture over the pineapple slices on both sides. Cover and leave to marinate for 30 minutes.

Place the slices of pineapple between a hinged grill and cook on a greased grid over hot coals for 10 minutes, basting with the marinade and turning after 5 minutes.

Serve the caramelized pineapple slices piping hot, accompanied by chilled double cream, if liked.

■ COOK'S TIP

Bananas barbecue beautifully and these are popular with adults and children alike. When serving to small children make some Chantilly cream omitting the rum and coffee or offer vanilla ice cream instead.

■ COOK'S TIP

To remove the central cores from the pineapple slices easily, press a small round pastry cutter firmly over the core.

223 CHERRY AND ALMOND FLAN

Preparation time:
20 minutes

Cooking time:
about 1 hour 20
minutes

Oven temperature:
200 C/400 F/gas 6

Serves 4-6

Calories:
509 - 339 per portion

YOU WILL NEED:
175 g/6 oz shortcrust pastry dough
50 g/2 oz margarine
50 g/2 oz caster sugar
1 egg
50 g/2 oz ground almonds
25 g/1 oz self-raising flour
few drops almond essence
450 g/1 lb canned cherry pie filling

Roll out the dough and use to line a 20 cm/8 inch loose-bottomed flan ring or a pie plate. Bake blind for 20 minutes and leave to cool.

Cream the margarine and sugar together and beat the egg well into the mixture. Stir in the ground almonds and sifted flour. Add the almond essence and mix well.

Spread the cherry pie filling in the baked pastry case and cover with the almond mixture, spreading carefully.

Bake in the preheated oven for about 1 hour or until firm and golden brown.

224 SPICE BISCUITS

Preparation time:
20 minutes

Cooking time:
15 minutes

Oven temperature:
180 C/350 F/gas 4

Makes 20 biscuits

Calories:
83 per portion

YOU WILL NEED:
150 g/6 oz plain flour
1 teaspoon ground cinnamon
1 teaspoon ground mace
100 g/4 oz butter
50 g/2 oz caster sugar

Sift the flour and spices together. Cream the butter and sugar together until light and fluffy, stir in the flour mixture and bind together with your fingertips.

Roll out on a floured board to a thickness of about 5 mm/¼ inch. Using a 6-cm/2½-inch fluted cutter, cut out 20 rounds. Place the rounds on a greased baking sheet and prick with a fork.

Bake in a preheated oven for 15 minutes. Leave the biscuits to cool on a wire rack.

■ COOK'S TIP

This flan tastes equally good either served hot or cold. If taking to a picnic, cover with cling film after it has cooled.

■ COOK'S TIP

This is a good basic biscuit recipe that can be varied by using different spices if liked. Different sizes and shapes of cutters can also be used.

225 NUT AND SULTANA BARS

Preparation time:	YOU WILL NEED:
15 minutes, plus	*100 g/4 oz digestive biscuits*
chilling	*50 g/2 oz plain sweet biscuits*
	50 g/2 oz walnuts, chopped
Makes 12 bars	*75 g/3 oz sultanas*
	2 tablespoons golden syrup
Calories:	*75 g/3 oz butter*
207 per portion	*50 g/2 oz plain chocolate*

Grease a shallow 18 cm/7 inch square tin.

Put all the biscuits in a polythene bag and crush with a rolling pin. Put the crushed biscuits in a bowl and mix in the walnuts and sultanas.

Melt the golden syrup, butter and chocolate in a heatproof bowl over a pan of hot water. Pour on to the biscuit and nut mixture and mix well. Spoon into the prepared tin and smooth with a palette knife.

Chill until set and then cut into bars.

226 CHOCOLATE SQUARES

Preparation time:	YOU WILL NEED:
15 minutes, plus	*175 g/6 oz plain chocolate*
chilling	*50 g/2 oz margarine*
	225 g/8 oz digestive biscuits
Makes 9 squares	*grated rind of 1 orange*
	100 g/4 oz sultanas
Calories:	*50 g/2 oz glacé cherries, chopped*
334 per portion	*5 glacé cherries, halved, to decorate*

Melt the chocolate and margarine in a heatproof bowl over a pan of hot water. Remove from the heat.

Put the biscuits in a polythene bag and crush with a rolling pin. Add the crushed biscuits to the chocolate mixture with the orange rind, sultanas and chopped cherries. Mix well and press into an 18 cm/7 inch square tin. Mark into nine squares and decorate with the halved cherries.

Chill well before cutting into squares.

■ COOK'S TIP

Replace the sultanas with the same quantity of chopped dates. Before use, dip the knife in cold water to prevent the dates sticking to it.

■ COOK'S TIP

Use half an orange to press the biscuit mixture into the tin evenly and smooth the surface. Any juice will be quickly absorbed.

227 MULLED PEARS

Preparation time:
15 minutes

Cooking time:
about 30 minutes

Serves 4

Calories:
103 per portion

YOU WILL NEED:
4 small ripe pears
4 teaspoons demerara sugar
16 cloves
4 tablespoons redcurrant jelly
grated rind of 1 orange

Peel, halve and core the pears. Place each pear on a square of foil. Mix together the demerara sugar, redcurrant jelly and orange rind. Spoon between the pear halves. Spike each with four cloves and wrap the foil around the pear, securing tightly at the top. Then wrap each pear parcel in another piece of foil.

Place the pears amongst the hot coals of a barbecue and cook for 30 minutes, or until tender. Serve hot with cream.

228 GOLDEN BAKED APPLES

Preparation time:
15 minutes

Cooking time:
20-30 minutes

Serves 4

Calories:
296 per portion

YOU WILL NEED:
4 cooking apples
50 g/2 oz butter
FOR THE FILLING
50 g/2 oz soft brown sugar
2 teaspoons ground cinnamon
25 g/1 oz walnuts,chopped
25 g/1 oz raisins

Core the apples and place each apple on a square of foil. Combine the filling ingredients thoroughly and fill the apples with the mixture. Dot the apples with the butter and wrap them in foil, covering them completely and sealing the parcels tightly. Then wrap each parcel in foil.

Place the apples amongst the hot coals of a barbecue, turning once or twice, for 20-30 minutes or until tender. Serve with whipped cream or ice cream.

■ COOK'S TIP

If you dip the pears in lemon juice to prevent them from discolouring, the parcels can be prepared in advance.

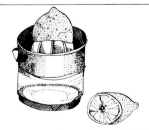

■ COOK'S TIP

As an alternative filling, combine 50 g/2 oz finely chopped dried apricots, 25 g/1 oz chopped stem or crystallized ginger and 50 g/2 oz soft brown sugar.

229 SATSUMAS WITH RUM AND RAISINS

Preparation time:	YOU WILL NEED:
20 minutes	*6 large satsumas*
	50 g/2 oz raisins
Cooking time:	*2 tablespoons soft brown sugar*
15 minutes	*3 tablespoons rum*

Serves 6

Calories:
65 per portion

Remove the peel from the top half of the satsumas using a sharp knife, carefully cutting around the circumference, just cutting the peel and not the fruit. Ease away the top half of the peel and discard. Remove the white pith from the fruit but leave the fruit intact in its orange peel cup.

Mix together the raisins and sugar and push into the centre of each satsuma. Pour a little rum over each. Place the satsumas on large squares of foil; bring the foil up around the fruit and twist to secure.

Place the satsumas amongst warm coals and cook for 15 minutes. Unwrap and serve with cream.

230 APRICOT-AND NUT-STUFFED FRUIT BREAD

Preparation time:	YOU WILL NEED:
15 minutes	*225 g/8 oz dried apricots*
	100 g/4 oz crystallized ginger,
Cooking time:	*chopped*
about 20 minutes	*50 g/2 oz unsalted butter*
	25 g/1 oz flaked almonds
Serves 8-10	*2 fruit loaves*

Calories:
386 - 309 per portion

Place the apricots, ginger and butter in a blender or food processor and process until the mixture is almost smooth. Stir in the almonds.

Slice the loaves at 2-cm/¾-inch intervals, cutting about three-quarters of the way through each time. Spread the apricot mixture between the slices of bread.

Wrap the loaves individually in foil with the shiny side inwards. Seal to make airtight parcels.

Cook over hot coals for about 20 minutes, turning the parcels occasionally. Unwrap and serve sliced with fruit salad.

■ COOK'S TIP

Other varieties of citrus fruit with loose peel, such as clementines, can be cooked in the same way. A complementary liqueur can replace the rum.

■ COOK'S TIP

A wide range of fruit loaves is available. The best type to choose for this recipe is one that is not too closely packed with dried fruit.

231 BUTTERSCOTCH DIP

Preparation time:
10 minutes

Cooking time:
about 10 minutes

Serves 4-6

Calories:
393 - 262 per portion

YOU WILL NEED:
75 g/3 oz butter
175 g/6 oz soft brown sugar
175 ml/6 fl oz evaporated milk
TO SERVE
apple wedges
banana slices
marshmallows
boudoir biscuits

Place the butter in a small pan and heat gently until melted. Add the sugar and half the evaporated milk and stir over a low heat until the sugar has dissolved. Blend in the remaining milk. Keep warm on the side of the barbecue.

Spear pieces of fruit or marshmallows on long-handled forks, or hold biscuits, and dip them into the butterscotch mixture.

232 CHOCOLATE FUDGE CAKE

Preparation time:
30 minutes, plus cooling and chilling

Cooking time:
40 minutes

Makes 1 x 20 cm/8 inch round cake

Calories:
Total calories: 1797

YOU WILL NEED:
100 g/4 oz butter
100 g/4 oz digestive biscuits, finely crushed
1 tablespoon golden syrup
225 g/8 oz caster sugar
2 tablespoons cocoa powder
2 tablespoons condensed milk
1½ teaspoons vanilla essence
50 g/2 oz flaked almonds, toasted

Put half the butter in a pan with the crushed biscuits. Heat gently, stirring, for 3-4 minutes, then press the mixture into a greased 20 cm/8 inch flan tin. Chill.

Add the remaining butter to the syrup, sugar and cocoa in a pan and stir in 2 tablespoons cold water. Stir over a low heat until the sugar has dissolved. Bring the mixture to the boil slowly, stirring constantly; add the condensed milk and boil for 6 minutes. Test with a sugar thermometer; the temperature should be at soft ball stage, (115-118 C/238-245 F). If it is not ready, repeat the test at minute intervals.

Remove from the heat, stir in the vanilla and whisk the mixture for 7½ minutes or until it is thickening slightly. Stir in the almonds then pour on top of the biscuit mixture. Smooth the top with a wet palette knife then mark into thin slices.

Leave to cool and set for about 4 hours. Chill overnight in the refrigerator.

▓ COOK'S TIP

For a chocolate dip, break up 100-175 g/4-6 oz plain chocolate and add to the hot butterscotch dip. Stir gently until the chocolate melts and the dip is smooth.

▓ COOK'S TIP

To test the mixture without a sugar thermometer, drop a teaspoonful into a bowl of iced water. Mould the mixture into a soft ball with your fingers and then take out of the water. It should not immediately lose its shape.

DRINKS

Long, cool drinks are the order of the day for both adults and children when it comes to summertime meals. Here are drinks with a dash of alcohol to suit adult tastes and drinks based on fruit to delight children.

233 FRUIT PUNCH

Preparation time:
10 minutes, plus chilling

Serves 4

Calories:
108 per portion

YOU WILL NEED:
150 ml/¼ pint sugar syrup
    (see Cook's Tip)
150 ml/¼ pint orange juice
150 ml/¼ pint pineapple juice
300 ml/½ pint cold weak tea
fruit slices (such as orange, lemon,
    pineapple, apple)
crushed ice
150 ml/¼ pint ginger ale
mints sprigs, to decorate

Pour the sugar syrup into a jug and stir in the fruit juices and the tea. Chill for at least 2 hours.

Add the fruit slices and the crushed ice. Mix well. Pour the punch into four tall glasses and top up with ginger ale. Decorate each glass with a mint sprig.

234 BLOODY MARYS

Preparation time:
5 minutes

Serves 8

Calories:
120 per portion

YOU WILL NEED:
350 ml/12 fl oz vodka
150 ml/¼ pint very dry sherry
100 ml/3½ fl oz lemon juice
1 litre/1¾ pints tomato juice
salt and pepper
1 tablespoon Worcestershire sauce
1 teaspoon Tabasco sauce
½ teaspoon celery salt
ice cubes

Mix together the vodka, sherry, lemon and tomato juices, stirring thoroughly, then add a little salt and black pepper.

In a screw-topped jar, shake together the Worcestershire sauce, Tabasco sauce and celery salt.

To serve, half-fill each glass with ice, top with the vodka and tomato juice mixture and then let everyone help themselves to the spicy mixture. Place a celery stick into each glass for stirring.

■ COOK'S TIP

To make the sugar syrup, place 50 g/2 oz granulated sugar and 150 ml/¼ pint water in a saucepan and stir over a low heat until dissolved.

■ COOK'S TIP

If serving iced drinks at a picnic, take the ice cubes in a wide-necked vacuum flask half-filled with water. This prevents the cubes sticking to the flask.

235 WHITE WINE PUNCH

Preparation time:
5 minutes, plus
chilling

Makes about
1.25 litres/2¼ pints

Total calories: 971

YOU WILL NEED:
1 bottle medium-dry, fruity white
wine
75 ml/3 fl oz cognac
75 ml/3 fl oz Cointreau
400 ml/14 fl oz soda water
large block of ice (see Cook's Tip)
2 tablespoons fresh lime juice
100 g/4 oz raspberries
1 peach, peeled, stoned and finely
sliced
8-10 lemon balm leaves

Chill the wine, cognac, Cointreau and soda water for at least two hours.

Place the ice in a large jug or punch bowl, pour in the wine, cognac and Cointreau and whisk. Add the lime juice, then the soda water, stirring continuously.

Float the fruit in the jug, decorate with the lemon balm leaves and serve immediately.

236 RED WINE CUP

Preparation time:
10 minutes, plus
chilling

Makes about
2 litres/3½ pints

Total calories: 520

YOU WILL NEED:
1 bottle red wine
200 ml/7 fl oz Framboise liqueur
1.25 litres/2 pints sparkling
mineral water
large block of ice (see recipe 235)
1 small cucumber, very thinly sliced
6 borage sprigs with flowers,
leaves roughly chopped
(optional)

Chill the red wine, Framboise liqueur and mineral water for 2 hours.

Put a large block of ice in a punch bowl or large jug, pour over the wine, add the Framboise and stir well. Pour in the mineral water, stirring constantly. Add the cucumber slices, chopped borage leaves and borage flowers, if using, stir once more and serve in wine glasses.

■ COOK'S TIP

Large blocks of ice melt more slowly than cubes, thus diluting the drink less and keeping the liquids cooler for longer. To make a block of ice, remove the *plastic divider from an ice-cube tray and freeze the water in that, or use a shallow plastic container of a similar size. Prepare the ice a day or two in advance.*

■ COOK'S TIP

Framboise is a raspberry-based liqueur. If it is not available, use 150 ml/¼ pint brandy and 3-4 tablespoons Grenadine as an alternative.

237 SANGRIA

Preparation time:
10 minutes, plus
chilling

Serves 4

Calories:
667 per portion

YOU WILL NEED:
300 ml/½ pint dry red wine
2 tablespoons brandy
4 tablespoons fresh orange juice,
*   strained*
300 ml/½ pint lemonade
FOR THE DECORATION
½ orange, thinly sliced
½ lemon, thinly sliced
1 dessert apple, cored and thinly
*   sliced*
ice cubes

Mix the red wine and brandy in a large jug. Add the strained fresh orange juice and the lemonade and stir well. Chill for at least 2 hours.

238 CHAMPAGNE-STRAWBERRY COCKTAIL

Preparation time:
5 minutes, plus
chilling

Makes about
900 ml/1½ pints

YOU WILL NEED:
175 ml/6 fl oz Fraise de bois
*   liqueur or strawberry liqueur,*
*   chilled*
1 bottle non-vintage dry
*   champagne, chilled*
strawberries, to serve

Total calories: 766

Pour the Fraise de bois into a large jug; add the champagne gradually, stirring continuously. Stir very gently to avoid losing the fizz.

Place a strawberry at the bottom of each glass, and top up with the champagne, pouring quickly but being careful not to let it overflow. Drink immediately.

■ COOK'S TIP

The brandy may be omitted, if preferred. Try replacing the orange juice with cranberry juice, which is available in cartons in most supermarkets.

■ COOK'S TIP

It's a nice idea to welcome guests with a cocktail or wine cup before sitting down to dinner. Choose this luxurious champagne-based cocktail, a fruity

White wine punch (recipe 235) or a sophisticated Red wine cup (recipe 236).

239 CHILLED CLARET CUP

Preparation time:
5 minutes, plus
chilling

**Makes about
1.75 litres (3 pints)**

Total calories: 647

YOU WILL NEED:
1 x 75 cl bottle young claret
½ bottle non-vintage port
150 ml/¼ pint brandy
large block of ice (see recipe 235)
5 tablespoons orange juice
3 tablespoons lemon juice
50 g/2 oz icing sugar
2 oranges, finely sliced
1 lemon, finely sliced
350 ml/12 fl oz soda water
6 sprigs fresh mint

Put the wine, port and brandy in the refrigerator and chill for 2 hours.

Wrap the ice in a clean tea towel and smash with a hammer until finely crushed.

Fill a large jug with the crushed ice, then pour in the claret, port and brandy and stir.

Put the orange and lemon juices in a small bowl, add the icing sugar and whisk with a fork for a minute to dissolve the sugar.

Add to the jug, with the slices of oranges and lemon. Pour in the soda water, stirring all the time.

Float mint sprigs in the jug. Serve the claret cup immediately in wine glasses.

240 BLACKCURRANT FIZZ

Preparation time:
10 minutes, plus
chilling

Cooking time:
20 minutes

**Makes about
2 litres/3½ pints**

Total calories: 647

YOU WILL NEED:
*400 g/14 oz blackcurrants, stalks
    removed, washed and drained*
6 tablespoons caster sugar
6 tablespoons lemon juice
*1.25 litres/2 pints fizzy lemonade,
    chilled*

Place the blackcurrants in a heavy-based saucepan over a low heat. Pour over the sugar and cook gently for 20 minutes, stirring once or twice, until the currant juices are plentiful.

Strain the blackcurrants, pressing them lightly to extract all the juice and discard the currant skins. Add the lemon juice and half the lemonade, whisking well together.

Pour the mixture into a large jug and chill for 30 minutes, then add the rest of the lemonade, whisking well. Return the Blackcurrant fizz to the refrigerator and chill until you are ready to serve it.

COOK'S TIP

Try to use mint with a more subtle flavour, such as apple or eau-de-cologne, rather than the more everyday spearmint.

COOK'S TIP

This makes an ideal drink for a children's picnic. Make it for teetotal adults, too, but use a sparkling mineral water instead of lemonade.

INDEX